THE
MAYANS

Other titles in the *Lost Civilizations* series include:

The Ancient Egyptians
The Ancient Romans
Empires of Mesopotamia
The Mayans

LOST CIVILIZATIONS

THE MAYANS

Stuart A. Kallen

LUCENT BOOKS
P.O. BOX 289011
SAN DIEGO, CA 92198-9011

Library of Congress Cataloging-in-Publication Data

Kallen, Stuart A., 1955–
    The Mayans / by Stuart A. Kallen.
        p. cm. — (Lost civilizations)
    Includes bibliographical references (p.) and index.
    ISBN 1-56006-757-8 (alk. paper)
    1. Mayans—Antiquities—Juvenile literature. 2. Central America—Antiquities—
Juvenile literature. 3. Mexico—Antiquities—Juvenile literature. [1. Mayans. 2.
Indians of Central America.] I. Title. II. Lost Civilizations (San Diego, Calif.)
    F1435 .K35 2001
    972.81'016—dc21

                                                                        00-010738

Copyright © 2001 by Lucent Books, Inc.
P.O. Box 289011, San Diego, CA 92198-9011
Printed in the U.S.A.

Contents

FOREWORD

"What marvel is this?" asked the noted eighteenth-century German poet and philosopher, Friedrich Schiller. "O earth . . . what is your lap sending forth? Is there life in the deeps as well? A race yet unknown hiding under the lava?" The "marvel" that excited Schiller was the discovery, in the early 1700s, of two entire ancient Roman cities buried beneath over sixty feet of hardened volcanic ash and lava near the modern city of Naples, on Italy's western coast. "Ancient Pompeii is found again!" Schiller joyfully exclaimed. "And the city of Hercules rises!"

People had known about the existence of long lost civilizations before Schiller's day, of course. Stonehenge, a circle of huge, very ancient stones had stood, silent and mysterious, on a plain in Britain as long as people could remember. And the ruins of temples and other structures erected by the ancient inhabitants of Egypt, Palestine, Greece, and Rome had for untold centuries sprawled in magnificent profusion throughout the Mediterranean world. But when, why, and how were these monuments built? And what were the exact histories and beliefs of the peoples who built them? A few scattered surviving ancient literary texts had provided some partial answers to some of these questions. But not until Pompeii and Herculaneum started to emerge from the ashes did the modern world begin to study and re-construct lost civilizations in a systematic manner.

Even then, the process was at first slow and uncertain. Pompeii, a bustling, prosperous town of some twenty thousand inhabitants, and the smaller Herculaneum met their doom on August 24, A.D. 79 when the nearby volcano, Mt. Vesuvius, blew its top and literally erased them from the map. For nearly seventeen centuries, their contents, preserved in a massive cocoon of volcanic debris, rested undisturbed. Not until the early eighteenth century did people begin raising statues and other artifacts from the buried cities; and at first this was done in a haphazard, unscientific manner. The diggers, who were seeking art treasures to adorn their gardens and mansions, gave no thought to the historical value of the finds. The sad fact was that at the time no trained experts existed to dig up and study lost civilizations in a proper manner.

This unfortunate situation began to change in 1763. In that year, Johann J. Winckelmann, a German librarian fascinated by antiquities (the name then used for ancient artifacts), began to investigate Pompeii and Herculaneum. Although he made some mistakes and drew some wrong conclusions, Winckelmann laid the initial, crucial groundwork for a new science—archaeology (a term derived from two Greek words meaning "to talk about ancient things.") His book, *History of the Art of Antiquity*, became a model for the first generation of archaeologists to follow in their efforts to understand other lost civilizations. "With unerring sensitivity," noted scholar C.W. Ceram explains, "Winckelmann groped toward original insights, and expressed them with such power of language that the cultured European world was carried away by a wave of enthusiasm for the antique ideal. This . . . was of prime importance in shaping the course of archaeology in the following century. It demonstrated means of understanding ancient cultures through their artifacts."

In the two centuries that followed, archaeologists, historians, and other scholars began to piece together the remains of lost civilizations around the world. The glory that was Greece, the grandeur that was Rome, the cradles of human civilization in Egypt's Nile valley and Mesopotamia's Tigris-Euphrates valley, the colorful royal court of ancient China's Han Dynasty, the mysterious stone cities of the Maya and Aztecs in Central America—all of these

and many more were revealed in fascinating, often startling, if sometimes incomplete detail by the romantic adventure of archaeological research. This work, which continues, is vital. "Digs are in progress all over the world," says Ceram. "For we need to understand the past five thousand years in order to master the next hundred years."

Each volume in the *Lost Civilizations* series examines the history, works, everyday life, and importance of ancient cultures. The archaeological discoveries and methods used to gather this knowledge are stressed throughout. Where possible, quotes by the ancients themselves, and also by later historians, archaeologists, and other experts support and enliven the text. Primary and secondary sources are carefully documented by footnotes and each volume supplies the reader with an extensive Works Consulted list. These and other research tools, including glossaries and time lines, afford the reader a thorough understanding of how a civilization that was long lost has once more seen the light of day and begun to reveal its secrets to its captivated modern descendants.

AN ENDURING LEGACY

Deep in the jungles of Central America stand some of the most magnificent ancient pyramids and temples ever constructed in the Western Hemisphere. Between approximately 400 B.C. and A.D. 900, the Mayans built these monuments and ruled over a great civilization in a region known as Mesoamerica, located on the Yucatán Peninsula in southern Mexico and in the present-day countries of Guatemala, Honduras, El Salvador, and Belize. During the course of more than twenty centuries, great Mayan cities such as Tikal, Copán, Chichén Itzá, and Mayapán rose from the tropical rain forests and then fell again into obscurity.

In addition to the temples, the Mayans constructed royal palaces, government buildings, and monuments covered with sculpture and intricate picture writing called hieroglyphs. They also developed a system of wells, canals, and reservoirs to provide drinking water to their people. And, although they did not use the wheel, the Mayans built some of the finest highway systems of any ancient people in order to facilitate commerce and trade throughout Central America. These brilliant Mayan accomplishments were achieved without the use of metal tools and without the help of work animals such as horses, mules, or oxen.

During the height of Mayan civilization, the people who lived in these cities were kings, priests, nobles, artisans, merchants, farmers, soldiers, and slaves. In the artwork of clay idols, vases, murals, and stone monuments, Mayan potters and painters left detailed records of royal dynasties that spanned centuries. And using only the naked eye, Mayan priests, mathematicians, and astronomers mapped out the intricate movements of the Sun, Moon, planets, and stars.

By the time the Spanish first came to the region in 1517, the Mayans had constructed a total of two hundred cities over the course of

The Pyramid of the Sorcerer, located in Uxmal, Mexico, is one of many structures built by the Mayans between approximately 400 B.C. and A.D. 900.

the centuries, about twenty of which contained populations of over 50,000. At the peak of Mayan civilization, between A.D. 600 and 900, an estimated 10 to 20 million people inhabited the region.

Hidden in the Forest

The Mesoamerica of the Mayans was bounded on the west by the Pacific Ocean and on the east by the Gulf of Mexico and the Caribbean Sea. Within this area, the Mayans thrived in an incredibly diverse, and often harsh, environment. The region contains cool, rugged, and dry regions in the highlands and humid, dense and tropical rain forests in the lowlands.

Because of the sizable level of rainfall in the lowlands—

up to 160 inches per year—rain forests quickly covered over buildings that fell into disuse over the centuries. By the time the Spanish arrived in Mesoamerica, much of the former glory of the Mayan empire lay smothered under a thick blanket of trees, roots, vines, ferns, and shrubs. Parrots, jaguars, and monkeys inhabited the regions that were once home to powerful kings and mystical priests.

Not until John Lloyd Stephens and Frederick Catherwood found the ruins of Copán in 1839 did the lost civilization of the Mayans become known to the outside world. Over the course of the next several years, Catherwood and Stephens discovered more than thirty-six separate sites, some so en-veloped by jungle that even the local people did not know of their existence.

Since that time, a steady stream of researchers, scholars, and others have visited Mesoamerica attempting to decipher the world of the ancient Mayans. As Gene S. and George E. Stuart write in *Lost Kingdoms of the Maya,*

Beginning in the . . . 1800s, hundreds of individuals ranging from the frivolous to the sober, from the eccentric to the ordinary, have worked to solve the mystery of the ruined cities. The key, as we now know, lies in scientific archaeology, yet that did not get under way in the Maya area until the late 1800s, when the discipline was in its infancy. Since then, methods have rapidly improved, and increased numbers of scholars and lay people have joined the excavators in the quest, including anthropologists, ethnohistorians, geographers, art historians, linguists, and epigraphists. In all, eight generations of experts from many nations have given us the story of people, time, and change in the land of the Maya.[1]

CHAPTER ONE

CITIES IN THE FOREST

Human beings have lived in Mesoamerica for at least 12,500 years, and scientists have dated Mayan pottery shards in the region to approximately 1500 B.C. The original Mayan people lived on the Pacific coast. In later centuries, as their populations grew, they began to move inland and build a greater number of cities. By around 1000 B.C, the Mayans supported themselves by farming maize (corn), hunting, and fishing. As populations increased, new villages were carved out of the forest, and a trade network developed between different regions. Over the centuries, this small Mayan society grew into the dominant civilization in Mesoamerica, overshadowing the Olmec and other large tribes in the region. In *Daily Life in Maya Civilization*, Robert J. Sharer describes the accomplishments of the Mayans at the height of their power:

> The great civilization of [the Mayans] flourished for over two thousand years, from about 400 B.C. until the Spanish began to conquer their lands in A.D. 1524. During that span a succession of independent kingdoms rose and fell across the varied landscape of the Maya homeland. The Maya population expanded into many millions

of people supported by a rich array of crops and the bounty of forests, rivers, lakes, and seashores. Their settlements ranged from small villages to large cities. The largest cities were capitals of the many Maya kingdoms. In each of these cities were elaborate temples, palaces, carved monuments, roadways, plazas, markets, and the many houses of their inhabitants. In times of peace the cities prospered from a network of trade that linked the independent Maya kingdoms. In times of war famous Maya kings led their people in the conquest of neighboring kingdoms. Captured warriors were adopted by the families of the victors, but the most important captives were sacrificed in religious ceremonies that celebrated each victory.[2]

Mayan kings left intricate chronicles of their accomplishments written in hieroglyphs and carved into stone monuments. Modern researchers continue in their attempts to unravel the mystery of these messages. Meanwhile, the Mayans have left many legacies to people in the present era, including foods such as maize, chocolate, and chili peppers. In addition, as Sharer

THE STUDY OF ARCHAEOLOGY

The secrets of ancient Mayan society have been revealed by archaeologists who have excavated buried cities in the rain forests and have cleared away centuries of jungle growth from the sites. In *Daily Life in Maya Civilization*, Robert J. Sharer explains the work performed by archaeologists.

"The study of past civilizations is a special concern of the field of archaeology (the science of past societies). Archaeologists have developed methods to recognize chiefdoms and preindustrial states from the remains these societies have left behind. These remains are known as the archaeological record. It ranges from artifacts (small portable items that can be moved or traded far and near) to permanent features (roads, buildings, fields, canals, temples, palaces, and settlements). Any concentration of artifacts and features defines an archaeological site; thus a site can range from a small hunting camp consisting of the remains of a cooking fire and a few hunting tools, to an entire city covering many square miles.

Artifacts and features are not the only remains used by archaeologists to reconstruct the past. Clues to ancient environmental conditions can help archaeologists determine the natural resources that were used and traded. Plant and animal remains tell them what foods were used to support an ancient society. For most preindustrial states, some of the best clues are found in recovered written records, because writing systems were often used to record the political and economic affairs of rulers and administrators."

Ancient Mayan artifacts such as this bowl provide archaeologists with information about early Mayan civilization.

The Pyramid of the Sorcerer (left) and the Governor's Palace (right) are located in the ancient Mayan city of Uxmal on the Yucatán Peninsula.

writes, the Mayans also created "great works of sculpture and painting; skillfully woven textiles; precious carved jades; sophisticated systems of mathematics; complex calendars; and beautifully proportioned buildings rendered in a variety of styles."[3]

Burning Sun, Drenching Rains

Many cities of the ancient Mayans were clustered on the Yucatán Peninsula, a relatively flat shelf of land that barely rises above the surrounding Gulf of Mexico. The northern lowlands area of the peninsula is home to the ancient cities of Uxmal, Chichén Itzá, Tulum, and others. T. Patrick Culbert describes the region in *Maya Civilization*:

The Mayan lowlands cover a large area: 96,500 square miles (250,000 square kilometers)—the approximate size of Pennsylvania, New York, New Jersey, and Massachusetts combined. South of the lowlands, the land rises steeply into the mountainous highlands of Guatemala and southern Mexico. This mountain zone is a tortured land, raked by several east-west mountain chains and their accompanying precipitous river valleys. Volcanic peaks, many still active, tower above the highlands, and earthquakes periodically devastate the land. To the south of the mountain chains, the land drops steeply toward the Pacific coast. The Maya still inhabit the highland country, as they did prehistorically. . . .

Mayanists traditionally divide the lowland area into northern and southern lowlands. . . . The northern section of the peninsula is flat, so that the Castillo (pyramid) at Chichén Itzá looks onto a vast tableland. This almost undifferentiated relief is broken near the peninsula's eastern edge by the low, rolling Puuc Hills—the location of an important group of ancient sites. Moving south into Guatemala, the land is marked by limestone ridges, flanked by depressions, that run on a northwest-southeast diagonal. Although the ridges are not high—a few hundred feet at most—they are fairly steep, with marked ecological differences between the ridgetops, the slopes, and the depressions. The large Maya sites are invariably located in the thin but well-drained soil atop the tallest ridges.[4]

The climate of Mesoamerica is hot and humid, with spring and summer temperatures averaging over ninety degrees in the day and winter temperatures cooling to the mid-eighties. The warm air is saturated with humidity during the rainy season, which lasts from May to December. While some areas of the Yucatán are relatively dry, receiving only about 20 inches of rain per year, to the south, the mountainous area of Guatemala is drenched with up to 160 inches of rain annually.

Around 1566 a Spanish bishop named Diego de Landa described the climate of the Yucatán:

The land is very hot and the sun burns constantly. There is, however, no lack of cool winds such as those from the northeast and east which blow steadily there, together with the sea breezes in the evenings. . . .

The winter begins on Saint Francis' Day [January 29] and lasts until the end of March, for at that time the north wind blows and gives the [native Maya] people bad colds and

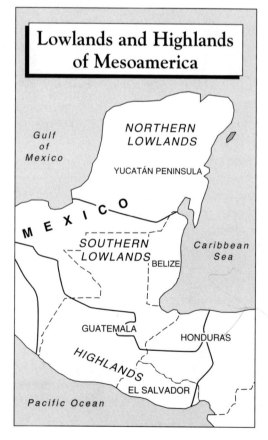

Lowlands and Highlands of Mesoamerica

Gulf of Mexico

NORTHERN LOWLANDS

YUCATÁN PENINSULA

M E X I C O

SOUTHERN LOWLANDS

BELIZE

Caribbean Sea

GUATEMALA

HONDURAS

HIGHLANDS

EL SALVADOR

Pacific Ocean

fevers because they are so scantily dressed.

Towards the end of January and February there is a brief summer with a burning sun; and during this time it only rains when there is a new moon.

The rain begins in April and lasts until September; and it is at this time that the Indians sow all the crops, which ripen although it never stops raining. They also sow a certain kind of maize (corn) which ripens around Saint Francis's [Day] and is harvested very soon after. [5]

Although it may rain there from April to September, the Yucatán is composed of porous limestone rock that absorbs most of the yearly rainfall. This leaves little water to flow into rivers or lakes. In the dry season there is little surface water. To overcome this problem in the Yucatán and elsewhere, the ancient Mayans built large reservoirs in areas with dense clay soils. The Tikal site in Guatemala is surrounded by ten such reservoirs that contain up to 40 million gallons of water. Farther to the north, the Mayans dug deep cisterns and lined them with plaster. In other areas, underground reservoirs were tapped for the water needs of the people.

Hurricanes are a constant threat in some regions of Mesoamerica and were a fact of life for the Mayans who lived there. These violent storms might have helped topple kingdoms by creating social unrest when villages and food crops were destroyed. In *The Well of Sacrifice*, Donald Ediger describes a destructive hurricane that passed through the Yucatán Peninsula in 1465:

On that winter day . . . a tidal wave heaved water onto the island of Cozumel on the east coast of the Yucatán Peninsula and winds brought foam from the sea onto the land and toppled the thatched huts. Weaker parts of temples and buildings fell from the impact of the wind or were quickly undermined by the torrents of water. The hurricane bent inland after striking Cozumel, leveling houses and buildings, felling trees and driving animals from their homes in the jungle. . . . At least one archaeologist believes the great storm of 1465 contributed to the abandonment of Uxmal and the further decline of the Mayan civilization.[6]

Dense Rain Forests

The Mesoamerican lowlands are covered with dense tropical forests as a result of the drenching rains. Giant hardwood trees such as mahogany and Spanish cedar tower up to 130 feet above the ground. Huge vines stretch between the trees, and brightly colored orchids grow in the forest canopy. The dense vegetation means that little sunlight reaches the ground, so little grows on the forest floor but the huge roots of the towering trees. The forests are alive with hundreds of animal species, as described by Sharer in *The Ancient Maya*:

[There] are anteaters, agoutis, pacas (large, edible rodents), and other food animals such as tapirs, brocket deer, and cottontail rabbits. There are also primates (howler and spider monkeys) and carnivores (the ocelot . . . and the largest New World cat, the

Dense tropical rain forests dominate the Mesoamerican lowlands.

jaguar). The ancient Maya held the jaguar in high esteem, especially for its pelt, which was symbolic of elite and ceremonial status. Bird life abounds: doves, parrots, woodpeckers, and toucans; and game birds, including quail. . . . But the quetzal, most prized of all, is found only in the highland rain forests. Reptiles and amphibians are also abundant: many species of toads, tree frogs, turtles, lizards, and snakes, including boas, racers, coral snakes, rattlesnakes, and the deadly pit viper, the fer-de-lance. . . . The rivers and lakes of the region provide edible snails . . . and fish such as the mojarra and catfish. . . . The lowland coasts abound with shellfish—shrimp, spiny lobsters, crabs—and sea turtles, which in ancient times were probably the single most important source of food from the sea. The manatee, or sea cow, is also native to the southern coasts, and . . . this large mammal also was used by the Maya. . . .

More often felt than seen are mosquitoes, gnats, fleas, ticks, chiggers, biting flies, wasps, and other stinging insects. The ancient Maya raised stingless bees as a source of honey, and their descendants continue to keep hives today.[7]

The ancient Mayans were well adapted to the harsh conditions of their environment, and they ingeniously utilized the infinite resources provided by the land. Mayan cities, for example, were constructed of the soft and malleable limestone that makes up the Yucatán. Veins of a hard flint-like rock called chert were found in the limestone, and this substance was used for tools. The dense rain forests, according to Culbert, "supplied a wealth of commodities: hardwoods for houses and furniture, boxes and trinkets, fuel; resin—from the copal tree—for ceremonial incense; dazzling plumes for the costumes of the elite; jaguar pelts for clothing, and fittingly, for the king's pillow covers."[8]

What the Mayans could not make, they imported from regions to the north and south through a network of trade routes, bringing in fish and salt from the coast, the black knife-making stone obsidian from the highlands, and pottery painting pigments, jade, and coral from various other regions.

Discoveries at Copán

By the time the Spanish arrived in the sixteenth century, the great Mayan kingdoms of old had already collapsed. The Mayans who still lived in the region were then forced to live under Spanish rule. It was not until the nineteenth century that American and European explorers were drawn to the tropics to unearth the secrets of the ancient Mayan past.

The work of uncovering the ancient Mayan civilization began in 1839 in the jungle wilderness in western Honduras in a valley known as Copán. On November 17, 1839, John Lloyd Stephens and Frederick Catherwood discovered a wall of cut stone nearly buried under a green carpet of ferns, shrubs, and trees. Stephens later described the discovery: "Soon we . . . [saw] a stone wall, perhaps a hundred feet high with [shrubs] growing out of the top, running north and south along the [Copán] river, in some places fallen, but in others entire. It had more the character of a structure than any we had seen. . . . I am entering abruptly upon new ground."[9]

The large wall described by Stephens was not made by nature but was part of the ruins later named the Acropolis, which had been abandoned by the Mayans around A.D. 800. The Acropolis had been constructed atop earlier temples, which themselves had been built on earlier buildings.

After the initial discovery, Stephens, an American lawyer, set about buying the site from a local man. Catherwood, an English artist, began to make dozens of sketches of the incredible statues and buildings at Copán. During their extensive exploration of the site, the two men discovered several roughly thirteen-feet-high free standing stone monuments called stelae (STEE-lee, the plural of stela), which were completely covered with intricate drawings. Stephens recorded the discoveries in his diary:

The wall was of cut stone, well laid, and in a good state of preservation. We ascended by large stone steps, in some places perfect, and in others thrown down by trees which had grown up between the crevices, and reached a terrace, the form of which it was impossible to make out, from the density of the forest in which it was enveloped. Our guide cleared a way with his machete, and we passed, as it lay half

During their exploration of Copán, John Lloyd Stephens and Frank Catherwood discovered many stelae such as the one shown here.

excite terror. The back was of a different design, unlike anything we had ever seen before, and the sides were covered with hieroglyphics. This our guide called an "Idol."[10]

Inspired by the ruins at Copán, Catherwood and Stephens would spend the next several years enduring innumerable hardships, including sickness and war, while searching the jungle for more Mayan ruins. They continued to push through the rain forests on foot, on mules, and in canoes, and eventually they discovered thirty-six different cities buried in the Mesoamerican rain forests, including the now-famous Palenque, Uxmal, Chichén Itzá, and Tulum sites.

When the two men returned home to write books about their experiences, they touched off a wave of exploration in the area. It was soon revealed that hundreds of sizable cities in Mesoamerica were built by the ancient Mayans, ancestors to the people who still inhabit the region today.

Piecing Together the Puzzle

Stephens's and Catherwood's efforts to understand the mysterious Mayan hieroglyphs were hampered by the fact that the hieroglyphs were written in several dialects of the Mayan language. (In modern times, Mayans speak twenty-eight different dialects of their language.) These hieroglyphs, according to *The Magnificent Maya,*

look like miniature works of art crammed into small squares; in fact, they are precise units of writing in a complex script, one of only five known independently created systems of written language. Their pic-

buried in the earth, a large fragment of stone elaborately sculptured, and came to the angle of a structure with steps on the sides, in form and appearance, so far as the trees would enable us to make it out, like the sides of a pyramid. Diverging from the base, and working our way through the thick woods, we came upon a square stone column, about fourteen feet high and three feet on each side, sculptured in very bold relief, and on all four of the sides, from the base to the top. The front was the figure of a man curiously and richly dressed, and the face, evidently a portrait, solemn, stern, and well fitted to torial quality allowed those familiar with the symbols to read them without much training and gave scribes scope to display their skills and creativity.[11]

Hoping to solve the riddle of their meaning, nineteenth-century scholars began searching in churches and libraries for Mayan historical documents that were written around the time of the Spanish conquest.

In 1863 Brasseur de Bourbourg, a French priest, found a copy of a work called *Account of the Affairs of Yucatán* (*Relación de las Cosas*

de Yucatán) at the Royal Academy of History in Madrid, Spain. The work was originally written in 1561 by Spanish bishop Diego de Landa. De Bourbourg found an abridged copy made in 1661 that, according to *Breaking the Maya Code* by Michael D. Coe, was "a gold mine of informed information on all aspects of Maya life as it was in Yucatán on the eve of the [Spanish] Conquest."[12]

De Landa's mission in the Yucatán had been to convert the Mayans to Christianity. In the meantime, the priest learned the Mayan language and began to record his observations of Mayan customs and culture. But de Landa was troubled by Mayan

Frederick Catherwood sketched this drawing and dozens of others during his expedition to Mesoamerica with John Lloyd Stephens in 1839.

spiritual beliefs. According to *The Magnificent Maya,*

> In a town . . . on the Yucatán coast, [de Landa] came across a cache of nearly 30 hieroglyphic books. They were lovely objects, their delicate calligraphy painted in black and red ink on paper made from the inner bark of the fig or mulberry tree . . . and covered with jaguar skin. Although these volumes could have proved a tremendous resource for his researches, de Landa's religious fervor came tragically to the fore. He [said that] since they "contained nothing [but] superstitions and falsehoods of the devil, we burned them all, which [the Mayans] took most grievously, and which gave them great pain."[13]

Three of the books, called codices, survived, however, and were eventually sent to European museums in Madrid, Paris, and Dresden. A fourth was later found in a cave in Mexico.

In the 1880s English researcher Alfred Percival Maudslay greatly advanced Mayan research. On seven different expeditions, Maudslay retraced the paths walked by Stephens and Catherwood to compile an amazingly accurate record of the architecture, art, and hieroglyphs of the Mayan ruins. Coe explains Maudslay's methods:

> To make this record, he used an immense wet-plate camera; the plates had to be developed on the spot. To make casts, he had to bring in all the materials necessary (plaster, papier mâché, etc.). All of this work, plus

the difficulty of setting up camps and supplying [his crew] with food, had to be done in the rain and the heat, in regions bereft of all but the most rudimentary trails.[14]

In the 1890s archaeologists from Harvard University's Peabody Museum began excavations at Copán. Mayan research was slowed during World War I (1914–1918), but the era from 1924 to 1960 is considered by some to be the golden age of Mayan research. During these decades teams of researchers from the Carnegie Institution, Tulane University in New Orleans, the British Museum, and others unearthed hundreds of ruins in Mesoamerica.

Cracking the Code

In spite of the work of researchers, the meaning of the Mayan pictographs remained hidden. A few symbols relating numbers and calendars were interpreted thanks to de Landa's texts.

In 1952 Yuri Knorozov, a Soviet linguist and expert in Egyptian hieroglyphs, discovered that the ancient Mayans used over three hundred different glyphs. In 1958 writing expert Heinrich Berlin added to the knowledge of Mayan hieroglyphs, and in 1960 Russian-born American researcher Tatiana Proskouriakoff deciphered dates that were attached to portraits of Mayan rulers. These discoveries allowed successive scholars to successfully interpret about 80 percent of Mayan glyphs. And, as Gene S. and George E. Stuart write,

> Our image of the builders of the ancient cities has changed dramatically since 1960. Some of the reasons lie in

THE HARDSHIPS OF EXPLORATION

Those who explored the Mayan ruins did so under extreme physical hardship. Disease was rampant in the hot, humid climate, and the rain forests were rife with stinging insects and poisonous snakes. In 1863 French photographer Désiré Charnay described coming under attack by huge bloodsucking insects called *piques*. His story was reprinted in *Lost Cities of the Maya* by Claude Baudez and Sydney Picasso.

"Night fell and I settled into my hammock, where I quickly fell fast asleep. But . . . I was suddenly awoken by dreadful pain. The sound of wings filled the room, and feeling around myself I found a multitude of cold flat insects the size of a large cockroach. It was horrific! Several of them were walking over my face; I hurriedly lit a candle, and my eyes were struck by the most revolting scene imaginable.

Over two hundred of the dreadful creatures lay trapped in my hammock . . . at least thirty of the animals were still attached to me, and I quickly shook them off; my face, hands, and body were covered with swellings that were unbearably painful. Several of the insects lying in the hammock were fat and swollen with the blood they had sucked from me; the walls were covered with their companions. . . .

I armed myself with a short plank of wood and embarked on the massacre. It was an appalling and disgusting task, which made me feel quite sick. The battle lasted two hours; without pity, without mercy, I squashed every one. Once I was sure that the place was clean, that there were only dead bodies left . . . I tried to go back to sleep; but two hours later I had to repeat the whole procedure. . . . The next day I changed my place of residence, but my enemies hounded me down there as well, and my life became a living hell."

the flood of hieroglyphic decipherments pioneered by epigraphists Yuri Knorozov, Heinrich Berlin, and Tatiana Proskouriakoff. These show that the inscriptions deal largely with the lives and careers of the rulers and members of their courts.[15]

Continuing Research

Since the 1960s research into the Mayan past has accelerated. Modern archaeologists have added computers and cell phones to their picks, shovels, and dirt strainers, and hordes of teachers, students, and researchers continue to unearth the secrets of the

Mayans. In the February 1993 issue of *National Geographic*, Arthur A. Demarest, a professor of anthropology at Vanderbilt University, wrote about an archaeological dig he oversaw in a remote area of northern Guatemala:

In 1989 we began to construct our own small town at [the ruins of] Dos Pilas which takes its name from two nearby springs. Thatch-roofed launches motored south from the town of Sayaxché on a two-hour

THE BOOK OF THE JAGUAR PRIEST

One of the few surviving texts written by the Mayans is the sixteenth-century *The Book of the Jaguar Priest*, or *Book of Chilam Balam of Tizimin*. The text was originally in Mayan, but it was translated to Spanish script and was recorded when the Spanish conquest was in progress. Researchers believe that the majority of the book was dictated to a bilingual scribe in secret by Mayan priests who were trying to record the knowledge in ancient codices before they were burned by Spanish missionaries. The book is not a linear history in the modern sense, but, according to Robert J. Sharer in *The Ancient Maya*, "the reconciliation of actual events with [Mayan] prophesy."

Before relating ancient Mayan prophesy, the first pages of *The Book of the Jaguar Priest* tell the story of the Spanish conquest, which began in 1517.

"Now in those days when Mayapán was captured in battle, they confronted the katun [year] of affliction. During the migration of the remnant of descendants . . . of Yaxum [the first father] a good fortune should have come to generation after generation of his sons; but instead there came all at once castigations, oppression, vigilance in the night. That was a long time ago.

With rivers of tears we mourned our sacred writings amid the delicate flowers of sorrow in the days of the katun. . . .

Although after the days of shooting down the multitudes we pleaded for mercy, [the Spanish] then kindled fires over the whole province. The heavens were sealed against us. . . . Should we not lament in our suffering, grieving for the loss of our maize and the destruction of our teachings concerning the universe of the earth and the universe of the heavens?"

Archaeologists continue to make important discoveries about ancient Mayan civilization.

trip up the Petexbatún River, bringing us metal roofing, heavy generators, computers, and other supplies. Then, from a portage at Lake Petexbatún, mules . . . pulled our provisions for five hours through dense rain forest to the camp. In a few months, we had a kitchen, dining hall, medical clinic, and fully functioning lab complete with computer and drafting workstations. . . . [Scientists] began studying thousands of potsherds [pieces of broken pottery], scores of monuments, bone fragments, spearheads, trash heaps,

and miles of fortifications of Dos Pilas and the half dozen Petexbatún cities it once dominated.[16]

Even though researchers have been excavating Mayan ruins for more than 160 years, new discoveries continue to be made. In 1997, in an area on the Guatemala coast rarely visited by archaeologists, researchers found several major sites dating back to 400 B.C. filled with stelae, altars, and other valuable ruins.

But the precious Mayan ruins that have survived centuries of decay in the tropical rain forest are facing new threats to their existence. Ancient artifacts are in great demand among collectors and fetch huge sums of money on the black market. In February 1998 looters broke into an ancient Mayan burial chamber in Copán and stole five jade statues and about two thousand jade and shell beads.

The ruins at Chichén Itzá face more serious problems. This city, abandoned around A.D. 1250, is now surrounded by modern oil wells and refineries that belch black smoke into the air. This pollution results in acid rain, which has permanently damaged Mayan monuments in the region. And swelling populations of land-hungry people in other regions are rapidly cutting down the valuable hardwood rain forest trees for fuel and lumber. In areas around Guatemala City, dozens of ancient sites buried under layers of dirt and forest have been destroyed, pushed aside in favor of houses, roads, and other buildings.

The secrets of the Mayans remained buried and unknown for centuries before their mysteries were revealed in modern times. Today Mayanists have entered a new battle—to save these valuable burial sites as yet unearthed before their enigmas are lost forever to the ecological destruction of the modern age.

CHAPTER TWO

THE CLASSIC MAYAN CIVILIZATION

The rise of Mayan civilization took place within a region originally dominated by other societies, most notably the Olmec and Oaxacan civilizations. The Mayans borrowed liberally from the surrounding cultures. The Oaxacan, for instance, invented a hieroglyphic writing system similar to one later adapted by the Mayans. The Olmecs developed intricate political and social networks, which the Mayans refined and expanded. In addition, Olmec and Oaxacan artists created huge portraits of their kings carved into stone, a practice that the Mayans would also imitate.

Archaeologists have divided Mayan civilization itself into four distinct periods. The preclassic period lasted from 1500 B.C. to around A.D. 250 and was an era in which the Mayans became skilled at cultivating crops and began building villages in the highlands and lowlands. In the late preclassic period, beginning around 300 B.C., the major cities of Tikal, El Mirador, and others began taking shape. This era saw the development of intricate celestial calendars and hieroglyphic writing along with the construction of grand

temples decorated with sculptures of Mayan gods and kings.

During the early classic period, from A.D. 250 to 600, Tikal and the nearby city of Uaxactún became the major powers in Mesoamerica, and Mayan society became divided along rigid class lines. A ruling class of kings and administrators oversaw the lower classes of artisans, farmers, and workers who made up the majority. The first known stela was carved in Tikal in A.D. 292, and in 378 that city conquered nearby Uaxactún. During this era, when new monuments or temples were constructed, the ceremonies were preceded by ritual human sacrifice.

The late classic period, from A.D. 600 to 900, saw an unprecedented wave of temple and palace construction. By 700, Mayan culture was at its peak as cities such as Copán and Palenque grew and prospered. Although the cities were culturally similar, they were fiercely independent, and there was often bloody intercity warfare. During this time the artistic talent of the Mayans also reached its zenith as buildings, music, pottery, clothing,

HUMAN SACRIFICE

The Mayans believed that life could only come from death, and rulers believed that sacrifice helped them maintain contact with the spirit world. Leaders sacrificed food, animals, or even human beings to dedicate a new temple or celebrate an important event. City residents did not sacrifice their own people but rather those captured in battle. In his sixteenth century book *The Maya*, Diego de Landa describes a sacrificial ritual.

"If they were to remove his heart, they took him to the courtyard with great ceremony and attended by a large company of people, and, having smeared him with blue [paint] and put on [a sacrificial] cap, they led him to the round altar, which was the sacrificial stone. After the priests and officials had anointed that stone with the blue color and driven out the [evil spirits] by purifying the temple, the [priests] seized the poor wretch they were going to sacrifice, and with great speed placed him on his back against the stone and held him by his legs and arms so that they divided him down the middle.

This done, the executioner came with a large stone knife and dealt him, with great skill and cruelty, a blow between the ribs on the left-hand side under the nipple. He then plunged his hand in there and seized the heart and, like a raging tiger, drew it out alive and, placing it on a plate, handed it to the priest, who went very hurriedly and anointed the faces of the idols with that fresh blood.

Sometimes they performed this sacrifice on the stone and high altar of the temple and then threw the body, now dead, down the steps of the temple."

A sacrificial altar from Tikal.

The Mayan arts, including pottery, flourished during the late classic period.

and other items became increasingly elaborate and finely crafted.

Around A.D. 900, the Mayan empire mysteriously lapsed into chaos in what is known as the postclassic period. The hieroglyphs that tell archaeologists so much about Mayan society mysteriously stopped—the last glyph in Tikal is dated 869. Although little is known about what caused the collapse, researchers have drawn several scenarios: the region became overpopulated; a severe drought caused crops to fail; political revolution broke out; or a major war destroyed much of the empire in the southern lowlands. The jungle quickly swallowed cities that were once the jewels of the Mayan empire as they were deserted by their people. Meanwhile, on the northern

Yucatán, the city of Chichén Itzá began to grow and assume some of the grandeur of the abandoned cities to the south. That city also fell around 1250, and by the time the Spanish arrived in the sixteenth century, all of the major Mayan cities had been abandoned by the people who once inhabited them.

Building Temples

Until the 1930s archaeologists had discovered few preclassic Mayan villages. These ruins were buried by newer cities that were built directly on the older ruins. T. Patrick Culbert explains: "The Maya lived in the same locations for centuries, constantly building larger and larger structures that demolished or buried earlier ones. Hence it was only through massive excavations—requiring huge investments of time and money—that the early periods could be properly investigated." [17]

A site called Cerros in Belize reveals the customs and ceremonies the Mayans used when they undertook the building of a new monumental city. Scientists speculate this pattern was repeated elsewhere as small villages grew into powerful urban centers. According to Culbert,

> At about 50 B.C., Cerros was only a cluster of pole-and-thatch huts near the water's edge, a simple fishing village as it had been for several centuries. Then, a great ceremony took place. A section of houses was leveled and covered with earth. Dishes from a ritual feast were broken, then scattered about; precious pieces of jade were crushed and added to the offerings, along with water lilies and the

flowers of fruit trees. Once the area had been thus cleared and sanctified, construction began. A masonry temple of three rooms was built atop a steep, two-tiered pyramid. Four giant tree trunks were set up inside the temple rooms, symbols . . . of the mythical trees the Maya thought held up the corners of the universe. Finally, four giant stucco masks—as at Uaxactún and Tikal—flanked the single stairway that rose to the temple. The masks formed a cosmological map. The bottom two, on the first tier of the pyramid, were snarling jaguar faces representing the Sun God—the rising sun to the east and setting sun to the west. Above them were masks of Venus—the morning star and evening star—hovering above the sun as they do in the sky. What rites took place in the temple we cannot know. Our best guess is that they may have insured the continued daily rise and fall of the sun, and the continued growth and replenishment of human beings and of corn.

This first temple at Cerros was not to stand alone for long. Soon a second, much larger, temple was erected, nearly in front of the first; this was followed by a third, then a fourth temple, each endowed with complex celestial imagery.[18]

The *Popol Vuh*

Although archaeologists and anthropologists have accurately uncovered the earthly origins of Mayan society, the Mayan people have their own creation story. This legend

was first recorded in writing by a sixteenth-century Mayan nobleman in Guatemala who learned the Roman alphabet from Spanish friars. A transcription of this book, known as the *Popul Vuh* (*Book of the Community*), was discovered in a Guatemalan library in 1854.

Like many other ancient people, the Mayans developed a complex religious ideology based on the belief that spirits, gods, and goddesses permeated every facet of life. According to Linda Schele and Mary Miller in *The Blood of Kings: Dynasty and Ritual in Maya Art*,

> [To the] Maya, the world was a complex and awesome place, alive with sa-

A Mayan sun god mask from Palenque, Mexico. The Mayans believed that spirits, gods, and goddesses permeated every facet of life.

cred power. This power was part of the landscape, of the fabric of space and time, of things both living and inanimate and of the forces of nature—storms, wind, smoke, mist, rain, earth, sky and water. Sacred beings moved between the three levels of the cosmos, the Overworld which is the heavens, the Middleworld where humans live and the Underworld of Xibalba [ze-BAL-bah], the source of disease and death.[19]

The first section of the *Popol Vuh* describes the failed attempts of the gods to form humans out of mud, wood, and rushes. In the second section, two divine boys known as the hero twins and named Hunapu and Xbalanque defeat the lords of the underworld in a ball game that resembles modern soccer. This complicated story is explained by Robert J. Sharer:

The father of the Hero Twins was also a twin. He and his brother were ball players who had played ball in Xibalba [the underworld] and then were sacrificed by the gods of death. The brother was buried under the Xibalba ball court; the father was decapitated and his head hung in a calabash tree. From the tree his head impregnated one of the daughters of the death gods by spitting into her hand. Fleeing this angry death god, the pregnant girl came to the earthly realm. There she gave birth to the Hero Twins, who grew up and discovered their father's old ball game equipment. Realizing their heritage, they followed their father and uncle by becoming such famous ball players that they too were

invited to play ball in Xibalba with the lords of the Underworld.

In Xibalba the gods of death subjected the Hero Twins to a series of daily ball games and nightly trials, but they outwitted the death gods each time. However, the only way they could escape Xibalba was by jumping into a pit of fire. After the death gods ground up their bones and threw them into a river, the Hero Twins were reborn and returned to Xibalba seeking revenge. They succeeded by showing the death gods an amazing feat. One twin decapitated the other, then brought him back to life. The death gods were so amazed by this that they demanded the Hero Twins to perform the trick on them. This is what the Hero Twins were waiting for, so they decapitated the gods of death but of course did not bring them back to life. Following their victory over death, the Hero Twins escaped from Xibalba and were transformed in the sky as the sun and Venus, destined to re-enact their descent into Xibalba and their escape and rebirth forevermore.[20]

The third section of the *Popol Vuh* details how the Mayans were successfully created out of corn by the forefathers named Tepeu and Gucumatz, who "began to talk about the creation and the making of our first mother and father; of yellow corn and of white corn they made their flesh; of corn meal dough they made the arms and the legs of man. Only dough of corn meal went into the flesh of our first fathers, the four men, who were created."[21]

The hero twins—mythic Mayan ball players that, according to legend, defeated the gods of the underworld—are carved on this cylindrical vessel.

The exploits of the hero twins are widely depicted in Mayan hieroglyphs, and researchers used the story as recorded in the sixteenth century to decipher the meaning of various pictographs related to the twins.

The Classic Mayan World

According to their intricate calendars, the Mayans believed that their world began precisely on August 13, 3114 B.C. But it was not until after A.D. 300—more than thirty-three centuries later—that what we call classic

Mayan society was in full flower. Culbert describes a typical Mayan city during this classic period:

Maya sites seem to adhere to no obvious plan—there are no grids of streets or blocks laid out at right angles. But there is, in fact, a plan that makes all Maya cities much alike in basic layout. Every large site consists of a series of architectural groups—often separated from each other by as much as half a mile—linked by broad paved causeways. In each group, the structures are arranged around open plazas, now often grassy or overgrown with tropical vegetation. In Maya times they were paved with dazzling white plaster that sparkled in the tropical sunlight. One plaza is usually recognizable as the most important because it contains the greatest number of stone carvings and is surrounded by the largest buildings. Temples tower above the main plaza, some solitary on giant pyramids, others whole groups that are clustered on a large platform. At one side of the plaza is a jumble of low stone buildings and courtyards, entered only by narrow passageways; these obviously were not meant for public traverse. Upright stone slabs called stelae, accompanied by round slabs called altars (perhaps mistakenly, because they simply may have been daises [raised platforms for public pronouncements]), stand in rows in front of temples. The carvings on the stelae most frequently show a single standing figure whose ornate costume fills the surrounding space. At the edges of the figure, or on the sides of the stelae, hieroglyphic inscriptions relate history.[22]

Classic Mayan sites were dominated by towering stone pyramids, and temples were often from 100 to 150 feet high—equal to

Towering stone pyramids with steep stairways are common in classic Mayan sites.

8 to 12 stories in a modern building. Steep, narrow stairways led up the front of each temple, and, according to Culbert, "their steps [were] too narrow for anything more than the ball of the foot—a misstep means an uninterrupted plunge to the plaza below. Maya priests . . . climbed these awful steps weighted down with unwieldy costumes and laden with gifts for the gods (and presumably praying with all their might)."[23]

These forbidding temples were used for religious purposes while nearby palaces acted as the homes and administrative buildings for

THE WORK OF PRIESTS

The duties to be performed by traditional Mayan priests ranged from the mundane to the incredible. They were spelled out in *The Book of the Jaguar Priest.*

"To impersonate and invoke the deity
to offer food and drink to the idols
to effect the drawing of the pebbles of the days and regulate the calendar
to read weather and other omens in the clouds
to study the night sky and interpret the appearances of the celestial bodies
to determine the lucky and unlucky days for various mundane activities by
    the casting of lots
to perform the numerous rituals of the cup, the plate, etc.
to work miracles
to concoct medicinal herbs into ceremonial drinks
to predict the future
to announce the times for various agricultural and other activities
to insure adequate rainfall
to avert or bring to a timely end famine, drought, epidemics, plagues of ants
    and locusts, earthquakes
to distribute food to the hungry in time of need
to cut the honey from the hives
to determine the compensations to be placed on the crossroad altars
to read from the sacred scriptures the future road of the katun
to design and supervise the carving of stelae, the manufacture of wood and
    clay idols, and the construction of temples
to construct tables of eclipses and . . . risings of planets."

Mayan kings. C. Bruce Hunter describes one such palace in A *Guide to Ancient Maya Ruins*:

The Palace, a complicated network of buildings, vaulted galleries, patios, courtyards, porticoes, and subterranean chambers, went through many alterations during its long occupancy. This imposing structure covers approximately an acre and is situated in a central area of the ceremonial center. . . . Although most of the Palace buildings are only a single story high, in the southwest corner is a tower four stories high. This tower may have been used as an astronomical observatory or as an observation post to announce the arrival of important dignitaries. The tower is unique among Maya edifices. Beneath the southern end of the Palace structures are subterranean quarters with many rooms, indicating an earlier occupation here. The present Palace structures were no doubt built over these subterranean rooms at a later time.

The west side of the Palace is flanked by a palatial stairway leading to a porticoed chamber. The piers between doorways . . . depict [in stucco relief] full human figures of the noble class of people (some may be dancers), dressed in ceremonial or courtly clothing. . . .

The Palace, like all buildings at Palenque, has a mansard-type [steep, sloping] roof which was completely stuccoed in bas-relief [rising only slightly from surrounding surfaces]

with delicately sculptured scenes representing rituals, ceremonies, deities, and other subjects. . . . Buildings were given added height by the addition of extremely high roof combs [stone structures resembling the teeth of combs].[24]

The Trajectory of Mayan Power

Even though archaeologists have been uncovering the temples and palaces of Mayan civilization for more than 160 years, it has only been since the late twentieth century that researchers have been able to read Mayan hieroglyphs and piece together the puzzle of Mayan history. Tikal, whose temples rise more than two hundred feet above the dense Central American rain forest, has revealed the most about the ancient Mayans. The hieroglyphs and stelae of the site were barely accessible to researchers until the Guatemalan government built a dirt runway near there in 1951. In 1956 more than one hundred archaeologists conducted an exhaustive research program at Tikal sponsored by the University of Pennsylvania. By 1971 workers had unearthed more than five hundred buildings and researchers were able to piece together a comprehensive record of the city's long history over one thousand years after its collapse.

Tikal began as a small farming village around 600 B.C. but developed into a powerful and populous city-state during the following centuries. By 100 B.C. the greater Tikal region contained about forty thousand people, and by A.D. 400 the region was a major independent city-state. The man who established the first royal dynasty there around A.D. 219–238 was named Yax Moch Xoc, a fact revealed by hieroglyphic inscriptions

The stelae at Tikal became accessible to researchers after the Guatemalan government built a dirt runway near the site in 1951.

that venerate him inscribed by the following thirty-nine rulers of Tikal.

Yax Moch Xoc was followed by Scroll Ahau (Lord) Jaguar, whose figure, according to *The Magnificent Maya*, "appears on perhaps the most famous stela ever discovered—the one bearing a Maya date corresponding with July 8, A.D. 292, the oldest example of Mayan dating on a monument, and the traditional marker of the commencement of the Classic period."[25]

Thirty years later Moon Zero Bird became the next ruler of Tikal. Sharer writes that Moon Zero Bird

is known from an incised jade celt (small plaque) bearing his portrait and the date of his "seating" as king in A.D. 320. The celt, known as the Leyden Plaque, shows the king in a royal costume holding the double-headed serpent bar, standing over the prone figure of a captive about to be sacrificed to sanctify his inauguration.[26]

During this era, other lowland cities of all sizes also carved portraits of their rulers in stelae. These cities were independent of one another, and warfare between them was common. Cities such as nearby Calakmul, Caracol, and Yaxchilán all grew in size and came into direct competition with Tikal. Sharer describes how Tikal swallowed its neighboring cities:

Before long, some cities began to grow at the expense of adjacent ones. One by one, Tikal's nearest neighbors stopped carving monuments, a sure sign that Tikal had taken them over by warfare and alliance. In war, the defeated ruler was sacrificed and a puppet ruler took his place. In alliance, the local ruler acknowledged the supremacy of the Tikal king, an event usually commemorated by the exchange of royal brides from the ruling families of each city.[27]

Mayan Warriors

Great Mayan cities rose and fell as a result of violent conquest—depicted in thousands of glyphs and sculptures. Great chiefs are shown holding war clubs and javelins, and in the act of bloodletting, sitting on the necks of prisoners, or holding captured warriors by the hair. In *The Ancient Sun Kingdoms of the Americas*, Victor W. von Hagen explains the many causes of war:

War was continuous. It could not be otherwise. There were contending city-states with no set boundaries; farmers by the very nature of their agriculture moved back and forth in trespass. Commerce was carried on, then as now, at friend or enemy's expense.

Ancient glyphs and sculptures reveal the prevalence of war in ancient Mayan civilization.

Slaves were important, and the only way to get them was in battle. Victims were needed for sacrifice, since an individual was not expected to immolate [sacrifice] himself for the gods if someone else was available.[28]

The nature of Mayan battle, however, differs from modern ideas about warfare. Mayan cities were not defended by moats or walls, which leads archaeologists to believe that most wars were fought by surprise raids and small battles rather than by all-out scorched-earth destruction as in modern times. In addition, the Mayans believed that it was the gods who decided who won and who lost each battle. As such, they expected priests to

converse with the deities to determine the best time and place to fight.

In some cases, warriors were average citizens whose livelihood depended on agriculture, and wars were usually fought only after the corn harvest was finished in March or April. Battles ended when the sun went down and survivors sat down to eat the meals prepared for them by their wives, who accompanied them to battle sites. Mayan wars were usually fought close to home, as soldiers needed to bring all of their own supplies. The task of carrying food and other provisions fell to the warrior's wife and slaves. In later centuries, the Mayans developed a specific warrior class whose only job was to fight battles.

Archaeologists believe the ancient Mayans preferred surprise raids and small battles to prolonged and highly destructive wars.

The Mayans fought with lances, clubs, daggers, and a three-pointed knife carved from shell known as a trident. The Aztecs introduced the Mayans to the bow and arrow in the ninth century and also to the *atl-atl*, a weapon that allows javelins to be hurled in rapid succession with great force. To protect themselves, warriors carried large shields and wore a type of quilted cotton armor hardened in salt brine. In *Everyday Life of the Maya*, Ralph Whitlock discusses Mayan warfare:

> For the Maya, the prime purpose of war was to capture, not to kill, the enemy. In particular, they wanted to capture the *nacom*, the enemy leader. Once he was seen to be taken, the battle was over. His army melted away, leaving him to be carried in triumph to his captors' city, there to be offered in ceremonial sacrifice. The same fate befell his officers and other persons of rank. Ordinary soldiers and their followers were enslaved.

> A short, vigorous campaign as favoured by the Maya could best be achieved by a surprise attack. In organizing this the Maya were adept. They prepared the ground well, with the aid of an efficient scouting service. Then, assembling in ambush, they suddenly charged, with a maximum of wild warriors, trumpets blowing, drums beating and whistles piping. The *nacom* and his subordinates were gorgeously arrayed, in magnificent feathered headdresses that greatly increased their apparent height, and wearing flashing jewellery (sic). A Mayan onslaught must

have been a terrifying experience for an unprepared enemy.[29]

The Rise of Copán

To the south of Tikal lay Copán, another major power center of the Mayan empire. Beginning in A.D. 426, Copán was ruled by a continuous dynasty for almost four hundred years. This political stability helped the city develop into a major power.

Archaeologists are aware of this long dynasty because of a huge stone altar, known as Altar Q, that contains portraits of sixteen members of the ruling dynasty, each sitting on a name glyph carved to resemble a throne. According to dates on the altar, in A.D. 426, king Yax-Kuk-Mo, or "Blue-Quetzal-Macaw," oversaw the building of the first major temple in Copán after the city had been inexplicably abandoned by earlier residents.

More than two hundred years after Blue-Quetzal-Macaw founded the royal family, Smoke-Jaguar, became one of the dynasty's longest-ruling kings. Also known as "the Great Instigator," Smoke-Jaguar ruled for sixty-seven years and was widely celebrated for his accomplishments. According to *The Magnificent Maya*,

> Smoke-Jaguar led Copán through a period of unprecedented growth, expanding its dominion farther than ever before—possibly through the kind of territorial warfare that had seen Tikal lay claim to Uaxactún. . . . Thousands of new settlers may have flowed into the Copán region during his tenure, the population perhaps increasing to as many as 10,000. The land surrounding the acropolis became choked with new temples and

residences for the elite, while in the outlining districts trees were felled and fields that had long been used for corn production were abandoned to make room for the swelling population. The peasantry was pushed outward, and as more and more of the arable land was consumed, some farmers were reduced to tilling the inhospitable slopes of mountainsides.[30]

Smoke-Jaguar's son Eighteen Rabbit became king in 695 and took control over an area that included around one hundred square miles of Mayan territory as well as surrounding settlements. Eighteen Rabbit's dynasty

A carving that depicts Mayan king Eighteen Rabbit, whose dynasty was marked by an increase in art and sculpture celebrating his rule.

was marked by an increase in the manufacture of art and sculpture that celebrated his rule. His dynasty came to an end when Cauac-Sky, a lesser noble of a nearby region, captured and beheaded him. This move weakened the power and prestige of Copán's central government. Nevertheless, the three-century-old dynasty founded by Blue-Quetzal-Macaw maintained rule over the Copán region until the late eighth century.

In 1988 excavations of the Copán area revealed that in A.D. 775, fifteen jaguars—one for every previous ruler—had been sacrificed by King Yax Pac and buried in a crypt.

Jaguars were important to the Mayans, who considered them to be protectors of royalty and intermediaries between the living world and the world of the dead.

These were the glory days for the ancient Mayan civilization, which took place during a period of war, starvation, and deprivation in Europe known as the Dark Ages. While Mayan warriors fought on battlefields outside of major cities, kings amassed great power and wealth over tens of thousands of average citizens whose well-ordered lives would have been the envy of peasants anywhere in the world at that time.

CHAPTER THREE

THE
DIVINE KINGS

Life was good to those lucky enough to be born into Mayan nobility during the classic period. With their high social standing determined at birth, Mayan royalty enjoyed the best food, clothing, housing, and trade goods available. In fact, entire cities such as Copán and Tikal were built around the palaces of the one hundred or so royal families who oversaw all religious rituals and

Mayan royalty, such as the king represented here, inherited their positions and enjoyed a life of privilege.

the administration of royal business. The nobles were surrounded by warrior chiefs, priests, and bureaucrats who were often relatives, and their social needs were met by teams of musicians, scribes, courtiers, and artists. In the December 1997 issue of *National Geographic*, George E. Stuart elaborates on the privileges held by Mayan kings:

> The Classic period rulers of Copán claimed descent from the sun and ruled by that right. They waged war, traded, commissioned monuments to themselves and their lineages, and presided over a kingdom of some 20,000 subjects. These ranged from farmers who lived in pole-and-thatch houses to the elite occupying the monumental palaces near the Acropolis. . . . [Private] royal ceremonies of vision quest and ancestor worship—accompanied by bloodletting or hallucinogens [drugs]—went on in the security of secret courtyards and rooms atop the Acropolis.[31]

In the ranks below king, other people served as governors of smaller towns and overseers of government functions. They are

DIVINE NAMES

Mayan kings had colorful names such as Smoke-Jaguar, Zero Moon, and Eighteen Rabbit. These names have been interpreted by archaeologists, who took them from name glyphs and translated them from Mayan to English. Some of the glyphs have obvious translations, such as Snake-Jaguar's glyph, which contains both a snake and a jaguar. Sometimes the names of rulers are written in Mayan—for instance, *chan* means "snake," and *balam* "jaguar"—so Snake-Jaguar is sometimes referred to as Chan-Balam.

There is some confusion over the names of kings because researchers who discover a ruler's name publish it as they interpret it. Others who come along later may decide the name means something else, and so write it a different way. The sixteenth ruler of Copán, for example, has been called, according to T. Patrick Culbert in *Maya Civilization*, "Yax Pac, Yax Sun-at Horizon, New Sun-at-Horizon, Rising Sun, Madrugada (Spanish for dawn), and First Dawn." To combat this problem, many researchers simply give rulers numbers, in this case, Yax Pac is now referred to as Ruler Sixteen of Copán.

pictured in glyphs and paintings along with royalty, but they are always portrayed as faithful servants to the rulers.

The Mayan nobility placed great value on bloodlines and heritage and believed that their deceased ancestors continued to aid and assist them. Paintings and glyphs of Mayan kings sometimes portray dead parents in the sky, handing down symbolic gifts to the ruler. And, according to T. Patrick Culbert, "Living kings accordingly paid great attention to their chosen heirs. . . . Several ceremonies were conducted for heirs apparent, attended by a variety of local and visiting nobles."[32]

Unimaginable Power

Over the years Copán has left the most revealing royal record of all of the Mayan sites. During four hundred years of construction, each Mayan king tore down parts of old buildings or constructed temples directly on top of them. To explore the site, archaeologists have dug over one and a half miles of tunnels beneath the main Acropolis, each passageway leading to a different era of political and religious influence in this Mayan capital. While doing this work, excavators have discovered several crypts containing the remains of Mayan nobility along with priceless jewelry, pottery, pelts, paintings, and feathers meant to aid the rulers in the next life.

Deep within the lowest levels of the Acropolis, archaeologists discovered the bones of a woman believed to be the wife of dynasty founder Blue-Quetzal-Macaw, and queen mother of the following fifteen rulers. Stuart describes the find:

> The remains of the noble lady had been placed upon a thick rectangle of stone. She had been richly attired and was wearing one of the most extraordinary arrays of jade ever found in a Maya tomb. Her bones, particularly the skull, appeared uncannily bright and red, for after death she had been coated with cinnabar, or mercuric sulfide, a substance sacred to the Maya. The red decoration may have signified the direction east, associated with the sunrise and, by extension, resurrection.

With the discovery of the woman's tomb, and with the huge entwined bird emblem signifying the name of the founder on the facade of the same structure, it soon became evident that this particular part of the Acropolis constituted . . . in effect a sacred stack of burials and buildings hallowed by the presence of one of the almost unimaginable power in the eyes of the inhabitants of Copán.[33]

The King's Cosmic Duties

The "unimaginable power" wielded by Mayan kings came from the widespread belief that they were the center of all earthly religious power and were in intimate contact

This stela is adorned with the image of an ancient Mayan king. Ancient Mayans believed that these kings were the center of all earthly religious power.

with the deities. The Mayans thought that the bodies of their rulers contained divine energy, and their clothing, personal items, and rituals were able to bring sacred powers to Earth. Just as Earth revolves around the Sun, the Mayans believed that their kings were the center of everything in the universe that was physical and spiritual.

On the earthly plain, Mayan kings governed almost every aspect of society and culture. A Mayan ruler supervised the development of technology to make advancements in warfare, made sure that enough food was grown to support his kingdom, and controlled the daily lives of his subjects through the rule of the law. The king and his advisers decided the times and dates when religious ceremonies would take place, maintained authority over trade routes, and told people when and where to go to war. The king gave power and privilege to his friends and ordered torture and assassination of his enemies.

Mayan rulers married only one woman, whom anthropologists call queen or lady. In addition to this wife, a ruler might have several concubines, or mistresses. Although women tended to play a lesser role in political affairs, there were at least two women rulers in Palenque and other instances where women ruled as equals with their royal husbands.

Royal Fashion

Ancient pictures of Mayan kings show fearsome men who resemble unearthly creatures clad in feathers, jewels, and the skins of animals. This cosmic look was carefully cultivated from birth. Flattened foreheads were considered a sign of beauty among the Mayans, and babies' heads were bound

THE MAYAN COSMOS

The Mayans depended on their kings to act as emissaries between the gods and the average citizen. In *The Blood of Kings: Dynasty and Ritual in Maya Art*, Linda Schele and Mary Miller explain the Mayan view of the cosmos.

"The Maya Universe . . . was a three-leveled structure, consisting of the Overworld, the Middleworld, and the Underworld. The Underworld was entered either through a cave or through bodies of standing water, such as the ocean or a lake. The Middleworld, the world of humankind, was oriented by the four cardinal directions, each associated with a tree, bird and color. The principal direction was east, the point of the rising sun; its color was red. North, the direction of the ancestral dead, was white. West was black and associated with death and the Underworld. South was yellow and the right hand of the sun. At the center stood an *axis mundi*, or central axis, which was most often shown as a great ceiba tree with a supernatural bird at its crown. The roots of the tree were in the Underworld, its trunk in the Middleworld and its branches in the Overworld. The souls of the dead and the supernaturals of the Maya cosmos traveled from level to level via this tree."

between two boards at the front and back of the skull. After several days, the soft cranial bones had set, and the head swept back from the nose and narrowed at a peak at the top for the rest of that person's life. Crossed eyes were also considered beautiful, and mothers would hang ornaments between the eyes from a toddler's hair to cause the baby to become cross-eyed.

Along with the flattened skull and crossed eyes, Mayan rulers plucked out facial hair, filed their teeth into fangs, scarred their faces and bodies with tattoolike patterns, used putty to make their noses look like bird beaks, and braided ornaments into their hair. They pierced their ears and elongated their earlobes until a large egg could pass through the hole. Nose rings were worn through the septum, and nostrils were perforated with large holes filled with wooden plugs or amber.

For daily wear, men of royal birth wore thin cotton loincloths with larger garments wrapped around their waists and buttocks while calf-length capes covered the torso. Women wore long, billowing dresses called *huipils*.

For rituals and important occasions, the jewelry and clothing worn by Mayan kings was as elaborate as possible. Fingers and toes were decorated with jade rings, wrists and ankles with jewels and ornaments. Lords wore jaguar-skin breechcloths that were as long as skirts, and belts were decorated with drawings of human heads. Headpieces could be as large—or larger—than the man himself, consisting of a huge wooden mask of a god, which made the king appear to have two heads. On top, the mask might sprout a kaleidoscopic array of brightly colored feathers, including the dazzling green feathers of the sacred quetzal bird.

Ancient Mayan headpieces, such as the one represented on this ceramic urn, were elaborate and often composed of feathers, wood, jade, and beads.

Davíd Carrasco vividly describes the dress and appearance of a typical Mayan king:

The Great Sun Lords were sacred, in part, because of the clothes they wore. They were carefully and richly adorned with arrays of brilliant and colorful objects made of wood, cloth, feathers (quetzal, macaw, parrot), shells, and stones (jade, pyrite, obsidian), which were transformed into belts . . . knee guards, bracelets, and large undulating headdresses often in zoomorphic [combined human and animal] styles. They also carried sacred bundles filled with objects representing the presence of the divinities. Once arrayed with these prestigious and potent objects, they hardly appeared human at all. They represented a sacred presence organized by cosmic symbols of very high status. Embedded in their costumes were images of myths, gods, and spatial domains. These royal persons were living cosmograms designed to inspire awe, respect, and obedience.

Let us focus on one typical, extravagant image of a ruler dressed, literally, to kill. The image of the ruler of Dos Pilas appears in frontal position with his head turned to the left. Our general impression is that we are looking at a human being who has been transformed into a fantastic series of circles, lines, waves, and images associated not only with high rank but also supernatural power. For instance the ruler has a fabulous, opulent headdress consisting of feathers, wood, jade, and beads organized by an animal image. The zoomorphic head is mounted directly above the face and lacks a lower jaw, so that the ruler's head emerges from the mouth of the animal. In some cases rulers had several animal heads constituting their headdress associated with war or bloodletting, fertility, or kingship, according to the ritual occasion. These headdresses symbolized the intimate relations between the powers of these animals and the royal person who obtained and wielded these awesome forces.[34]

The costumes of kings and queens were fraught with symbolism and meaning. According to Linda Schele and Mary Miller,

> Costume and regalia are not only symbols of rank, wealth and prestige. They are the conduits and instruments in which sacred power is accrued. The person of the king, the clothing he wore, the symbols he hung on his body, the objects he manipulated—all these were directly connected to the Maya perception of the cosmos.[35]

Life in the Royal Court

Dressing in elaborate costumes was only part of the courtly life of Mayan rulers, whose daily life consisted of eating, drinking, religious rituals, and ceremonial celebrations.

Murals painted in the eighth century at Bonampak, Mexico, near the Guatemala border, show over two hundred separate individuals engaged in a very important ceremony—the presentation of an infant prince as the next heir to the throne. The murals, discovered in 1946, show the heir-designation ritual, and others show events that followed. Schele and Miller write,

> [The] paintings begin with a scene that shows the gathering of the royal family and lords who witness the presentation of a young heir seated on a throne. This presentation apparently motivates all the festivities that follow. In the next scenes, the king and two companions dress in ritual garb for a celebration that takes place 336 days after the child was presented to

Members of the ancient Mayan royal court sometimes included musicians (pictured) and artisans.

the court. . . . The fourteen witnesses in white mantles at the presentation of the child heir are identified in glyphs with the title *ahau* or "lord." *Ahau* is also a title carried by kings, and it is one of the highest titles recorded in Maya inscriptions. Some of the substantial lords, who display a girth that may also suggest a life of physical ease and epicurean [gourmet] habits, may have the right to rule city-states independently. Nevertheless, they have come to Bonampak to confirm the legitimacy of the heir of their peer, King Chaan-muan. This group also includes ranking males of the Bonampak lineage, who attend rites legitimatizing the little heir. . . .

Like squires of the court, sixteen young men, simply clad, assist the principal lords, including Chaan-muan, in donning their ceremonial dress. . . . Masked entertainers to the left of the principal lords perform and play musical instruments in the festival. . . . At the right of the Bonampak king and his two companions stand another group of nobles whose costumes are characterised by an orange color and an odd "bowler" hat suspended in their headdresses. They are identified by the common title of *cahal*, a governor or subordinate lord.[36]

As the Bonampak murals show, the Mayan court was busy with hundreds of people who assisted the king and queen and their heirs. In addition to administrators and visiting nobles, members of the court might consist of poets, artists, musicians, scribes, and other artisans whose official duties included recording the events in the court in song, poem, sculpture, painting, and art.

Gods and Monsters

The dress and fashion of Mayan kings made them living works of art, and they were immortalized in paint, stone, clay, and shell, as well as on stelae and walls of public buildings. Kings commissioned works of art to exhibit their great power to average citizens and to depict the ruling families in the best possible light. As such, Mayan artists depicted kings as rulers of the physical world and the Mayan cosmos. According to Schele and Miller,

> The proper order of society, the role of the king, commoners, and nobles alike, was expressed in permanent public form through art. Imagery described the cosmos, the origin of supernatural power and how to manipulate it, the reason for the existence of human beings, and their place in the cosmos. Ritual was conceived as the bridge between the supernatural and the mundane worlds, and the king was the agent of power who made the transaction from the sacred to the mundane.

Thus, Maya art depicts the historical action of civil kings, but those kings acted with sacred authority and supernatural power.[37]

The cosmos ruled by the kings, as depicted in Mayan art, contained a wide variety of gods and monsters. Some of these creatures, called anthropomorphs, were shown as having both human and animal characteristics. Others, called zoomorphs, resemble birds, deer, or jaguars, but with features added from other animals and exaggerated appearances that give them a fearsome, monsterlike quality. As Schele and Miller explain, "Zoomorphs often have distinct head types: these include a ubiquitous [common] head with a long nose, dragons derived from both lizards and snakes, and jaguar-based heads with comparatively short snouts. Deer, fish, snakes, crocodiles, birds, and human bodies are merged with these zoomorphic heads."[38] Such symbols, combined with portraits of kings, allow archaeologists to understand the supernatural powers claimed by individual rulers.

Ritual and Bloodletting

The Mayans believed that gods, monsters, and dead ancestors could enter the physical world and interact with the kings. For this to happen, however, it was necessary to shed the blood of kings—the passageway to the physical world was believed to be through a wound in the human body.

Bloodletting was an extremely common occurrence in ancient Mayan society. Royal blood was shed at weddings, when children were born, at funeral ceremonies, and on religious holidays. Even political events,

Zoomorphs have the features of many different animals, and are often exaggerated to give them a fearsome appearance.

crop planting, and the dedication of new buildings called for the spilling of blood. In the sixteenth century, Spanish bishop Diego de Landa described this practice:

They offered sacrifices of their own blood, sometimes cutting pieces from the outer part of their ears. . . . At other times they pierced their cheeks or lower lips, sometimes they sacrificed parts of their bodies, and at others they pierced their tongues at a slant through the side, passing through the hole some pieces of straw, which caused them great suffering. At other times they slit the superfluous part [foreskin] of the virile member [penis].[39]

Mayan women conducted their own bloodletting rituals. At the ceremonial site in Yaxchilán on the Guatemala-Mexico border, a series of carved horizontal beams, called lintels, depict the bloodletting ceremony of Lady Xoc aided by King Shield Jaguar. They are described by Carrasco in *Religions of Mesoamerica*:

In the first scene we see the king, Shield Jaguar, holding a huge torch above his ritual partner, Lady Xoc. Both are dressed in exquisite cos-

After bloodletting ceremonies, the ancient Mayans burned blood-soaked cloth in clay ovens, like this one, called braziers.

tumes decorated with cosmic designs. Notable are the shrunken head of a past sacrificial victim on Shield Jaguar's headdress, the beaded necklace with its Sun God pectoral hanging from his neck, highback sandals made of jaguar pelts, and a cape with designs of the four world directions. Jade ornaments encircle his knees and wrists, and his loincloth carries the ancestral lineage emblem. The shrunken head signifies his role in nurturing the gods through sacrifice. Lady Xoc wears a fabulous *huipil* woven in a diamond pattern with star designs and a skyband border symbolizing heaven and particular astronomical events. Her headdress is decorated with tassels and a head of the rain god Tlaloc out of which feathers spring. Most important she is pulling a thorn-lined rope through her tongue. The rope falls into a woven basket, which contains paper with spots of blood on it. Her cheeks have scroll designs signifying the blood she is giving to the gods. . . .

[Female] blood, shed in this sacrificial manner opens the membrane between heaven and earth through which flow astronomical influences, the spirit of ancestors, and legitimate power for a ruler ascending the throne.[40]

Bloodletting Ceremonies

Besides thorns, Mayan rulers used the spines of stingrays as well as obsidian and flint lancets in order to open wounds on their bodies. These lancets were sacred and were often carved with the elaborate image of the

RITUAL DRUG USE

While Mayan nobility often relied on hunger and blood loss to stimulate visions, they also used various drugs for ritualistic purposes.

The Mesoamerican region is home to over a dozen types of narcotic and hallucinogenic substances. Unlike many other pre-Columbian indigenous American cultures, the Mayans drank alcoholic beverages, including *pulque*, made from fermented corn and agave cactus juice. To prepare for rituals the Mayans sometimes drank *balach*, a drink fermented from honey and the bark of the balach tree. A very strong wild tobacco—much more potent than that grown today—was smoked to induce trances.

The Mayans also ate some of the many species of hallucinogenic mushrooms that grow in the region. Their names have been recorded in such descriptive terms as "underworld mushroom" and "lost-judgment mushroom."

Through trade, the Mayans are believed to have also acquired peyote cactus from the Aztecs to the north and coca (cocaine) leaves from the Inca lands to the south, although this is only speculation by researchers.

perforator god, who oversaw bloodletting rituals. Blood was dripped onto cotton or a paper cloth made from the bark of the fig tree. Because the Mayans believed that the gods could only consume the blood in the form of smoke, the blood-soaked cloth was burned in a charcoal-laden clay oven called a brazier.

Bloodletting ceremonies often called for the participation of hundreds of people in the open plaza of the palace. Dancers, musicians, and other performers began the ceremonies while dozens of people might participate in the actual bloodletting. Those participating would have prepared for the ritual by taking steam baths and fasting for days. The king and queen would enter, he would open a wound on his penis while she pierced her tongue. As their bodies went into shock from the massive loss of blood, they sometimes had highly valued hallucinations of gods and ancestors. Likewise, numerous others, weakened from lack of food and exposure to steam, would become hysterical, stumble about and faint, or experience wild hallucinations. As the blood-drenched cloths were burned in large braziers, columns of billowing black smoke formed what was called the vision serpent, a potent symbol of bloodletting often portrayed in Mayan art.

Prisoners of War

The Mayans believed that their gods required blood, and it was not only rulers and nobility who were called on to provide that substance. The Mayans left behind dozens of detailed paintings and sculptures in which prisoners of war were depicted as sacrificial victims. Captives are shown held by the hair or kneeling in front of kings, their mutilated bodies leaking drops of blood.

As depicted in various scenes, prisoner bloodletting was often a grisly, drawn-out process. An important prisoner, such as a king, might be kept alive for years, his only purpose in life to provide blood for the gods. And the Mayans practiced grotesque torture on these victims, such as lopping off fingers, ears, and noses; breaking bones; and cutting off scalps. One particularly gruesome ritual involved plucking the victim's still-beating heart from his chest as he watched.

This ancient Mayan ceramic vessel is decorated with a representation of the bloodletting dance.

Victims of sacrifice and bloodletting are never shown alone; they are always with the victorious king. When a king died, he was often buried with clay figurines that showed the victories he had in life. These figurines show tortured and tormented people screaming in pain, having their organs removed, and being set on fire.

Schele and Miller explain the reasoning behind the gruesome treatment of prisoners:

> The . . . elaborately recorded sacrifice of captives was a necessary component of many rituals in the cycle of dynastic life. [Rituals of accession to the throne], for example, required the offering of at least one human captive. Such offerings not only satisfied the constant demands by the gods for repayment of the blood debt incurred by man at his creation but tested the mettle of the new king as well. Perhaps the lineage even demanded proof of the physical prowess of the new lord before his installation in office could proceed. . . . To be a king, he had to take captives in war. Once made king, he was in jeopardy of becoming the most valued booty of his enemy. To sustain his rule, a king would not only have to fight off his foe, he would also attempt to capture and humiliate his enemy.

> It is striking that in the representation of warfare in their art, the Maya addressed no issues of material gain. Instead, they cast warfare and sacrifice in terms of ritual that upheld the cycle of kingship.[41]

The Death of a King

The history of the Mayans was recorded by triumphant kings who defeated their enemies and possessed enough wealth to commission murals and stelae that continue to inform the world of their victories. For lesser Mayan kings, however, life was short due to sacrifice, warfare, sickness, and natural catastrophe. As such, the significance of death in ritual and art was almost as important as that of war and conquest.

The Mayans believed that after death the soul traveled to a world called Xibalba, a sort of hell. The name comes from the word *xib*, roughly meaning "place of fright," and indeed, Xibalba was an awful place that contained decaying bodies and was believed to be the source of all disease on Earth. In other aspects, Xibalba resembled Earth—what the Mayans called the Middleworld—with buildings, trees, and temples ruled by the lords of death. Schele and Miller describe the inhabitants of Xibalba, called Xibalbans:

They include anthropomorphs, zoomorphs, animals and skeletal creatures of the most distasteful countenance. Many of the leading Xibalbans are shown with very old, toothless human visages, and some are transformational, combining male and female features. Xibalbans are named for the various causes of death, such as disease, old age, sacrifice and war, and are often depicted with black marks, representing decaying flesh, as well as bony bodies and distended bellies. Their jewelry consists of disembodied eyes that come complete with the hanging stalk of the optic nerve. Xibalbans are pictured emitting farts so pungent that they emerge in huge scrolls, and their breath is so foul it is visible. *Cizin*, one word for "devil" still used today by Yucatec speakers, literally means "one who farts."[42]

The *Popol Vuh* recounts the journey to Xibalba made by the hero twins, who descended a steep staircase and crossed a river of blood to arrive at the five houses of torture:

There were many punishments in Xibalba; the punishments were of many kinds.

The first was the House of Gloom, Quequma-ha, in which there was only darkness.

The second was Xuxulim-ha, the house where everybody shivered, in which it was very cold. A cold, unbearable wind blew within.

The third was the House of Jaguars, Balami-ha, it was called, in which there were nothing but jaguars which stalked about, jumped around, roared, and made fun. The jaguars were shut up in the house.

Zotzi-há, the House of Bats, the fourth place of punishment was called. Within this house there were nothing but bats which squeaked and cried and flew around and around. The bats were shut in and could not get out.

The fifth was called Chayim-há, the House of Knives, in which there were only sharp, pointed knives, silent or grating against each other in the house.[43]

The adventures of the hero twins were often painted on pieces of pottery that accompanied kings to their graves so that the king, like the hero twins, could confront the lords of death in Xibalba and escape from the underworld to a place where the pain and suffering of life was replaced by an abundance of food and drink.

In this heavenly spot, the sacred ceiba tree provided shelter and a place to rest forever from the hardships of labor. Mayan kings, queens, and priests were guaranteed a place in this paradise, as were women who died in childbirth and anyone who was killed in battle or sacrificed to the gods.

Since the Mayans focused on the journey to Xibalba and the escape from the underworld, there is little art that depicts the final ascent to heaven. As Schele and Miller write,

> The finale of the journey after death, the soul's triumphal exit from Xibalba,

was a clearly defined concept to the Mayans; however, because most funerary objects were designed to accompany the dead into the tomb and aid in the struggle in the Underworld, this last episode in the journey was only rarely depicted.[44]

For all of the dozens of Mayan rulers who have left detailed records of their accomplishments in stone, thousand of others died unknown, victims of war and sacrifice, their journeys to Xibalba made without maps etched in clay. Regardless of the circumstances of their death, however, Mayan kings and their royal families enjoyed unprecedented earthly rewards during their time in the Middleworld, the earthly paradise of palaces, temples, and ceremonial sites constructed by Mayan citizens who worshiped them as they did the gods.

Chapter Four

LIVING BY THE STARS

The Mayans had the most highly developed system of math, calendars, and astronomy of any people in the Americas, and indeed, almost anywhere in the world. These intricate systems served both cosmic and practical purposes. The Mayans believed that time, numbers, and the movement of the planets were ruled by supernatural gods. By keeping extremely accurate records on calendars, Mayan rulers believed that they could communicate with the gods, understand and evaluate events around them, and even gaze into the future. Respected scholar Sir Eric Thompson states that the Mayans' "skill with numbers developed because accurate calculations were important to divination. They developed astronomical observation to support astrology—a basic element in their religious beliefs."[45]

Driven to understand the gods, the Mayans developed an elaborate mathematical system—they were the first people in the world known to use the concept of zero. This allowed the Mayans to use place value to write numbers as people do today. For example, they could write the number *320* using a zero to hold the place of the ones. This remarkable academic feat made possible other developments in architecture, astronomy, and calendrics. In an article in the December 1975 *National Geographic*, Howard La Fay comments,

> [The] Maya practiced an astronomy so precise that their ancient calendar was as accurate as the one we employ today; they plotted the courses of the celestial bodies and, to the awe of the faithful, their priests predicted both solar and lunar eclipses. They calculated the path of Venus—an elusive planet that is by turns a morning and evening star—with an error of only 14 seconds a year.[46]

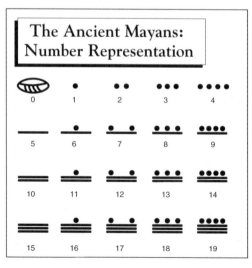

The Ancient Mayans: Number Representation

THE MAYAN NUMBER SYSTEM

The Mayans wrote numbers using a notation system based on three symbols, the bar, dot, and shell. The dot (•) was equal to one, the bar (—) had a numerical value of five, and the shell ⟨shell⟩ had the value of "completion" or zero. Using this system the number 3 would be written •••. The number 7 would appear as •• (5 represented by the bar, plus 2 represented by dots). The number 12 would have two horizontal bars representing five, topped by two dots representing one.

Instead of basing their number system on a base-ten, or decimal system, as is done in modern times, the Mayans based their system on base-twenty, or vigesimal system, possibly because twenty is the total number of human fingers and toes. Michiel Berger explains this system on the Maya Astronomy Web Page: "Because the base of the number system was 20, larger numbers were written down in powers of 20. We do that in our decimal system too: for example 32 is 3 x 10+2. In the Maya system, this would be 1 x 20+12, because they used 20 as base."

The place value went from bottom to top as opposed to right to left as in the modern system. The bottom layer of numbers represents multiples of 1s the second layer multiples of 20, the third layer multiples of 400, and the fourth layer multiples of 8000.

8,000s	
400s	••
20s	•
1s	•
	826

To write 826, the Mayans would place the 5 bar and 1 dot equaling 6 on the bottom. In the next position, the 1 dot equals 20. Next up, the two dots represent 2 x 400, or 800. Read from the top to the bottom, 800+20+6=826. Although this system might seem strange at first, it is comparable to the system of numbers written today.

The Mayan Calendar

While the Mayan numeral system was somewhat complicated, their calendar system was incredibly intricate and was used for the extremely difficult task of astrological divination. Each day and number on the Mayan calendar was associated with a specific deity, and that god or goddess held direct influence over that day. To further obscure matters, the Mayans used three separate calendars—the sacred round, or sacred almanac of 260 days; the solar calendar, or Vague Year of 365 days; and the Long Count, which did not repeat for 5,128 years.

While the average citizen might have understood the basic concepts, the complex calendar system was fully understood only by

The Mayans, known for their advanced calendar system, constructed this calendar column located in the Yucatán Peninsula.

a few. This knowledge remained a closely guarded secret among Mayan rulers, who used their ability to predict eclipses and other celestial events as proof of their supernatural powers.

The Mayans based their calendar numbering on a system that counted in intervals of twenty, known as the vigesimal count. The basic single unit—one day—was called a *kin*, which means "sun," "day," and "time." The next unit was twenty *kins*, or a *uinal*. The word *uinal* comes from *uinic*, the Mayan word for "human," because of a human's twenty fingers and toes.

Instead of going to 400 units, as in the numbering system, the Mayans used an important number called the *tun*, which was 360 days—not 20 *uinals*, but only 18. This was necessary to create a number closer to the actual solar year of 365.25 days.

The Mayans did not stop with a unit representing one year. The units are explained by Robert J. Sharer:

	1 kin, or 1 day	
20 kins	=	1 uinal, or 20 days
18 uinals	=	1 tun, or 360 days
20 tuns	=	1 katun, or 7,200 days
20 katuns	=	1 baktun, or 144,000 days
20 baktuns	=	1 pictun, or 2,880,000 days
20 pictuns	=	1 calabtun, or 57,600,000 days
20 calabtuns	=	1 kinchiltun, or 1,152,000,000 days
20 kinchiltuns	=	1 alautun, or 23,040,000,000 days [47]

56

The Sacred Count

The 260-day Sacred Count, or count of days, was made up of 20 day names and 13 numbers. Days had names such as Imix, Ik, Aknal, Kan, Chicchan, Manik, Oc, and Caban. This calendar was used to determine days of religious ceremonies and served as a basis for prophesies. Although the reason the Mayans used a cycle of 260 days remains unclear, according to an article by Berthold Riese in the *UNESCO Courier*, "in interviews with Guatemalan diviners . . . German ethnologist Leonhard Schultze Jena found that the number of days in the year matches the length of human pregnancy."[48] This system was tied to babies in another way. The designated deity for each day was believed to influence any child born on that day. As Alfredo Barrera Väsquez of the Yucatán Insitute of Anthropology and History explains,

When a baby was born, the parents took the child to a priest who, with the aid of star charts and books, would predict its future. Each day, each moment was governed by a different god; depending upon the exact time of birth, a child would owe a lifetime of devotion to the ascendant deity.[49]

OMENS FROM THE CALENDAR

Each day was unique under the Mayan calendar system, and priests believed that they could determine good and bad omens and predict the future from each day. *The Book of the Jaguar Priest*, written by Mayan shamans in 1593 after the Spanish Conquest, gives examples of those predictions:

1 IX	unlucky	In which death comes to men.
9 Ik	unlucky	There will be sickness.
1 Manik	lucky	The guilt of our sons unites us.
6 Eb	lucky	Searching the forest for deer.
1 Ahau	unlucky	Rain appears in Chacmitan.
7 Cimi	lucky	In which there is much rain.
12 Chuen		The culpability of our priests.
1 Ben	unlucky	Sickness; heat.
5 Caban		Blame falls on the seers.
8 Ahau	unlucky	Then comes our enemy Satan.
11 Akbal		The sin of our religion.
12 Kan		The sin of eating men.

In fact, until puberty, a child was named only for the day he or she was born. For instance, if a girl was born on 2 Caban that was her name until she married.

The Sacred Count was not divided into months or *tuns* but was a continuous count of 260 different days, each made unique by fixing a number from 1 to 13 in front of the 20 day names. Sharer explains:

> [The] calendar thus began: 1 Akbal, 2 Kan, 3 Chicchan, 4 Cimi, and so on. The fourteenth day name, Cib, at this point bore the number one that Akbal had borne the first time around; next came 2 Caban; and so on to 7 Ik. Following 7 Ik was 8 Akbal for the second time through the sequence of day names. . . . Not until every one of the thirteen numbers . . . had been attached in turn to every one of the twenty day names . . . was an almanac cycle complete.[50]

The entire 260-day unit was called a *tzolkin*, or Sacred Year.

The Vague Year Calendar

The Mayans' Vague Year, or *haab*, most resembles the modern calendar of 365 days. This calendar was composed of eighteen 20-day months or *uinals*, and a short 5-day month known as Uayeb, which allowed the Vague Year to accurately measure the solar year. Some of the month names were Pop, Zip, Tzec, Yax, Mac, Pax, Kankin, and Cumku. The days of the short month of Uayeb were considered unlucky, and people spent those days worrying about misfortune befalling them.

The glyphs shown here represent the eighteen 20-day months, or uinals, of the ancient Mayans' Vague Year Calendar.

The first month of the Vague Year is Pop, and the last month is Uayeb. But the last day of the year is not known as 5 Uayeb but rather as 0 Pop because the Mayans believed that the influence of Pop was already felt by the end of the year. New Year's Day was still written as 1 Pop.

The Mayans meshed the 260-day calendar with the Vague Year calendar in a system resembling a small wheel (the 260-day calendar) within a large wheel (the Vague Year calendar). Gene S. and George E. Stuart explain:

> At some point after the invention of the Sacred Round and the Vague Year, a scheme was devised to link the two together into an even larger cycle. Because of the mathematics involved, the combination of the

260- and 365-day cycles results in a grander cycle of 18,980 days—about 52 solar years. Within this cycle, which Mayanists call the Calendar Round, each single day bears a twin label—its Sacred Round number and name, and its number and name in the Vague Year. For example, project the Maya calendar forward to January 20, 1993 . . . and it falls on the Calendar Round date of 7 Akbal 6 Muan.[51]

The Long Count Calendar

While the calendar round was adequate for measuring up to fifty-two years, the time-obsessed Mayans went even further. In order to give an exact name to any date in the past, present, or future, the Mayans devised the Long Count calendar. As the Stuarts write, "Brilliant in concept, yet relatively simple in its mechanism, this invention allowed the Classic Maya to tame eternity with an absolute chronology in which any given date was unique."[52]

With the Long Count calendar, the Mayans were among the first societies in the world, according to Sharer, to use "a fixed point in the past from which to count their chronological records, and thus to give each day in the long span of time a unique designation."[53] Different societies have different starting dates for their calendars. A well-known example is the Gregorian calendar used in the United States, Europe, and elsewhere, which begins with the birth of Christ more than two thousand years ago.

The Mayans believed that the present world began after the last world came to an end, on the date archaeologists have determined to be August 13, 3114 B.C. On this date the great cycle of 13 *baktuns*—1,872,000 days or about 5,128 years—began. According to that theory, the ancient Mayans believed that the world would end on December 21, 2012.

The Long Count calendar has been invaluable to archaeologists piecing together Mayan history because they have been able to determine exact dates of important events registered in dated glyphs, stelae, and paintings. T. Patrick Culbert explains the intricate system of Long Count dating:

Many inscriptions on stelae begin with what is called an Initial Series, a long and abstruse dating formula commemorating the date on which the stelae was dedicated. The formula begins with a large Introductory Glyph, saying, in effect, "Here comes a date." Then comes the Long Count—indicating the year—followed by the position that the day in question has reached in the 260 cycle. Next come references to three other cycles whose intricacies are beyond our scope: first, the name of the "Lord of the Night"—one of nine gods who shared a nine-day cycle of their own; second, an entry specifying the position of the moon; third, an indication of the position in an additional cycle of 819 days (sometimes omitted, this cycle must have had numerological significance, as it fails to correspond to any astronomical phenomenon). Finally, the inscription acknowledged the position that the day occupied in the 365-day cycle. Once inscribed in its entirety, this Initial Series date served as a base for further calculations: Most other dates referred to in the same stela are indicated by instructions to count forward or backward a specified number of days from the base date. After all, who can blame the Maya for taking the odd shortcut? [54]

As complicated as the stelae dating process may seem, Mayan calendars had practical as well as cosmic purposes. In an agrarian society, farmers relied on calendars to know when to plant and harvest their crops. Priests used them to predict when the rains might come, and sailors used them to determine tides, full moons, and other necessary

data. The people who understood the movements of the calendars and their divine meaning were held in high esteem by the Mayans, as Maud Worcester Makemson notes in *The Book of the Jaguar Priest*:

It must be inferred that a rather formidable hierarchy of priests was required to regulate and interpret the calendar and advise and order the lives of the Maya people. The priests who had charge of counting the days were called Ah Pop and Ah Zam, which can be rendered "he who represents authority (pop)" and "he who works wonders (zam)."[55]

Glyphs Representing the Nine Deities of the Underworld

First

Second

Third

Fourth

Fifth

Sixth

Seventh

Eighth

Ninth

Mayan Astronomy

The Mayans used detailed astronomical calculations to devise their intricate calendars—and to maintain their religious belief system. The Mayans believed that the Sun, Moon, stars, and planets were gods who, if observed, would help them to ward off disaster, understand the destiny of their dynasties, pick the right time to go to war, discern the best time to plant crops, and even choose the best date for royal marriages. But the Mayans did not believe the cosmos was a benevolent place. As Linda Schele and Mary Miller write,

The Maya believed the universe to be a place filled with beings and forces that were dangerous and volatile if not contained with the proper rituals. They did not explain the movements of the stars and planets through the heavens with the cool mathematics of orbital mechanics, but as living beings moving against the backdrop of a living cosmos. Celestial bodies were the visible manifestations of the Hero Twins and gods of all sorts. The darkening of the sun in an eclipse was perceived as a form of dying from which the sun might not recover, and the first appearance of the Evening Star [Venus] was taken as a signal of war. The Maya had tables for predicting eclipses and the cycle of Venus, and [kings] made it appear as though [they] controlled these events.[56]

The Mayans left these detailed records written in a few surviving codices and carved into dozens of monuments, temples, and palaces. The details of recording precise astronomical events are discussed by John B. Carlson in the March 1990 issue of *National Geographic*:

To [Maya] astronomers . . . the sun traveled around the earth. Observing its shifting rise on the horizon, they were able to mark time and predict the future. Thus someone looking east from the Maya site of Uxmal could create a 365-day calendar by noting the swing of the sunrise from spring equinox (usually around March 20) to the first zenith [overhead] passage some 60 days later, to summer solstice

on June 21, the sun's farthest northern reach. Moving south, the sun again hits the zenith, then the fall equinox (September 23) before its southern extreme, winter solstice (December 22). These maximum excursions laid out earth space into four parts.

The Maya based a 584-day ritual calendar on an idealized cycle of the planet Venus: After a 236-day appearance as the morning star . . . it disappears for 90 days before shining in the west as the evening star for 250 days. Eight days later it is in the east again. [57]

The royal palace at Uxmal, mentioned by Carlson and known as the House of the Governor, is one of many major structures built by the Mayans to accurately align with cosmic events. Although the rest of the buildings in Uxmal are aligned on a north-south axis, the House of the Governor faces southeast. And, as Carlson writes, "it sights across a pyramid three miles distant to the horizon spot where Venus would have risen at its maximum southern excursion as the morning star about A.D. 900, when the structure was completed."[58]

The king who ordered the building of the palace is named after the rain god Chac, as the two hundred stone mosaic masks of Chac that adorn the palace attest. The king, according to Carlson, "added a special touch. The lower eyelids of each mask are carved with a glyph representing Venus the god of war and blood sacrifice to the Maya."[59]

Celestial Architecture

The Mayans were known to arrange the buildings in their cities to align with the

The House of the Governor at Uxmal was built by Mayans to accurately align with cosmic events.

Sun, Moon, and planets as they rose, set, and traveled across the sky. At the Mayan site of Chichén Itzá on the Yucatán Peninsula, built during the postclassic period, the four-sided pyramid known as El Castillo is adorned with staircases on each side. When the sun sets on the spring and fall equinoxes, the light and shadow cast on the stairs appears as a serpent slithering up the staircase from a stone serpent head near the bottom. The four stairs of the pyramid each contain 91 steps. When the top platform is added, the total number of steps equal 365—the number of days in a year.

Another building on the site is a round stone temple that looks like an ancient rendition of a modern observatory. This building, known as the Caracol Observatory, is equipped with a spiral staircase that winds up to a small room near the top where Mayan

astronomer-priests and kings could hold rituals and observe the sky. Through the small western window it is possible to see the setting sun only on March 21, the vernal equinox. The setting of the moon may be observed from other windows. As Sharer writes, "The places where the Mayan lived, from the smallest house to the largest city, were conceived of as symbolic representations of the universe. . . . From such associations, their inhabitants reaped the security and benefits of living in a sacred and properly ordered place."[60]

At the Tikal site, this concept has been observed in the placement of the buildings archaeologists call the Twin Pyramid Groups. These buildings, constructed for *katun-*, or, twenty-year-ending ceremonies, each represent the Mayan vision of the cosmos. Sharer continues:

The pyramids on the east and west represent the earthly plane and mark the cycles of time, specifically the birth and death of the sun. The nine-doorwayed building on the south represents the nine-layered underworld. And the walled enclosure on the north, open to the sky, represents the celestial domain, a fitting place for the stela and "throne stone" of the sponsoring ruler to reside.[61]

COMPLEX COSMIC CALCULATIONS

The Mayans were masters of cosmic calculation long before cultures in other parts of the world were capable of similar observations. This is discussed by Berthold Riese in "The Star System," an article in the November 1993 issue of the *UNESCO Courier*:

"The astronomy of the Mayas was not limited to observation of the stars and approximate predictions of the movements of the heavenly bodies. Using their sophisticated numerical systems and various tabular calculations in conjunction with the hieroglyphic script, Mayan astronomers were able to perform complex calculations with figures running into millions.

Their efforts were focused primarily on the sun and the moon. Different year lengths were used for different sorts of calculations. Normally they took the conventional 365-day year as a basis. However, years with a length of 364 days are also encountered, as are years of 365 1/4 days, similar to our own Julian calendar. The moon played a prominent role in stone inscriptions, which often begin with a day number followed by the phase of the moon and the day's position in a calendar of six lunar months.

Mayan astronomers also calculated the synodic period [relating to the conjunction of celestial bodies] of the planet Venus, and the figure of 584 days at which they arrived is astonishingly close to the modern astronomic value. But they went still further. A set of tables in the Dresden Maya codex cites correction factors to allow for the fractional deviations from this value, which can only be observed after decades and even centuries. Researchers also suspect that the Mayas were familiar with the synodic period of other planets, such as Mars and Jupiter, but this has not been proved conclusively."

The Caracol Observatory at Chichén Itzá, used by Mayan astronomer-priests to hold rituals and view the stars, resembles modern observatories.

Each of these ceremonial buildings was built at the end of a *katun*, or twenty-year, period. One altar at the site is dated 8 Ahau 8 Ou—the date archaeologists have translated as March 18, 692. The ceremony held on this date might have been typical of the elaborate rituals displayed on such holy cosmic days. The Stuarts describe the formal procedure:

> The ceremony for Katun 8 Ahau . . . must have been a sight to behold, a splendid pageant accompanied by the moaning intonations of conch-shell trumpets and wooden horns, against the staccato click of rattles and bone rasps and the deep cadence of wooden and clay drums. . . . While thousands watched from the plaza, the celebrants, including members of Tikal's highest ranking families, moved from station to station amid clouds of aromatic resin incense, pausing at each for the prescribed chants and recitations. . . . At high noon, the culmination of the ritual, [king] Ah Cacao, alone, entered the stone enclosure on the north side of the plaza, leaned his staff against the wall, and with appropriate solemnity, drew blood from his penis with an obsidian lancet. This act of bloodletting reaffirmed, for the whole of the katun to come, the link between Ah Cacao and the sacred calendar that regulated the lives of his people.[62]

After such ceremonies, Mayan kings commissioned stelae to commemorate the event. These stelae showed the kings outfitted in the full regalia of their ceremonial costumes, which were decorated with sacred signs such as the world tree. And, as Michiel Berger writes on the Maya Astronomy Page website,

> Their headdresses contained the Principal Bird Deity, in their arms they held a so-called ceremonial bar that represented the double-headed serpent of the ecliptic. By wearing the costume elements of the World Tree the Maya ruler linked himself to the sky, the gods and that essential ingredient, life. In addition, it has been found that when the [katun] ending coincided with certain planetary positions the Maya went to war to obtain captives.[63]

The Influence of the Sky Gods

According to Mayan belief, when the sun set, it traveled into Xibalba, the underworld. Each night the sun battled the lords of the underworld in a series of cosmic ball games, as the hero twins had done in the *Popol Vuh*. The intricately carved stone lid of the sarcophagus, or tomb, of King Pacal at Palenque is rife with imagery representing this concept. The huge lid measures seven by twelve feet and rests on a sarcophagus decorated with seven portraits of Pacal's ancestors. On the lid, Pacal is shown teetering on the edge of the earth, and then falling into the jaws of the underworld, into the mouths of two great dragons. Pacal is sitting on the symbol of the sun, known as the quadripartite monster. As Pacal falls, he pulls the sun into the underworld with him. Schele and Miller explain:

> Pacal falling . . . is equivalent to the sun at the instant of sunset. Like the sun, which rises after a period of darkness, he will rise after his triumph over the Lords of Death. . . . The king sited [the sarcophagus] along the line . . . with one of the most important alignments of the sun in the tropical year. At the winter solstice [December 21], the sun reaches its southernmost point, setting exactly on the line that runs through the tomb. Thus, the sun falls into darkness, into the Maw of the Underworld, through Pacal's tomb, confirming the symbolic imagery of death. . . . Just as the sun begins to move northward following the winter solstice, the dead, after the defeat of death, will rise from Xibalba to take up residence in the northern sky, around the fixed point of the Northern Star. . . . Just as the sun returns from the Underworld at dawn, and as it begins its northward journey after the solstice, Pacal has prefigured his return from the southbound journey to Xibalba.[64]

Along with the quadripartite monster, another important sky god was Itzamna, lord of the heavens, day, and night, who is often associated with the Milky Way star galaxy. Itzamna, often shown as an old toothless man, was the patron saint of Ahau, the last and most important day of the twenty-day *uinal*. Itzamna is also believed to have invented writing and books and to have given names to the various places in the Yucatán.

The Mayans sometimes depict Itzamna as a two-headed serpent; his right head facing east, representing the rising sun, his left head

THE MILKY WAY WORLD TREE

The galaxy of stars known as the Milky Way was very important to the Mayan people. On the Maya Astronomy Page website, Michiel Berger explains its significance.

"The Milky Way itself was much venerated by the Maya. They called it the World Tree, which was represented by a tall and majestic flowering tree, the Ceiba. . . . The World Tree was erect when [the constellation] Sagittarius was well over the horizon. At this time the Milky Way rose up from the horizon and climbed overhead into the North. The star clouds that form the Milky Way were seen as the tree of life where all life came from. . . . A major element of the World Tree include the Kawak Monster, a giant head with a kin [sun sign] in its forehead. . . . A sacrificial bowl on its head contains a flint blade representing sacrifice, and the Kimi glyph that represents death. The Ecliptic is sometimes represented as a bar crossing the major axis of the World Tree, making a form that is similar to the Christian Cross. On top of the World Tree we find a bird that has been called, the Principal Bird deity, or Itzam Ye. There is also evidence that shows the Sun on the World Tree as it appeared to the Maya at Winter Solstice.

During the months of winter, when the so-called 'Winter' Milky Way dominates the sky, it was called the 'White Boned Serpent.' This part of the Milky Way passed overhead at night during the dry season. It is not brilliant like the star clouds that dominate the sky North of the equator during the months of Summer, but observers at dark locations will easily see the glow. Here the Ecliptic crosses the Milky Way again, near the constellation of Gemini which was the approximate location of the Sun during Summer Solstice."

The Milky Way was important to the Mayans, who called it The World Tree.

facing west to greet the morning star, Venus. In his many manifestations, Itzamna was invoked for various ceremonial events involving calendars and celestial occurrences. During the Mayan New Year, Itzamna was called on to bring good luck; in the month of Uo, priests consulted with him to help predict coming events; and in Zip, he was asked to heal the sick and prevent disease.

Mayan beliefs were unique combinations of detailed religious viewpoints and exacting science. Berthold Riese writes about the priests who specialized in mathematics and cosmic divination:

> [Mayan] calendar experts constantly strove . . . to predict the future and connect the present with historical dates. In this way they could also learn something about the destiny of their clients—the ruler and private individuals.

These practical goals often served as a springboard for complex calculations and research which transcended their original purpose. For example, some of their calculations were projected so far into the past or future that the primary purpose must have been to quench the calendar

An eighth-century Mayan sculpture of the head of the sky god Itzamna.

priests' own thirst for knowledge and desire to explore the limits of their mathematical system. It is therefore reasonable to assert that the Mayas, like the Babylonians, Greeks, Arabs and Indians before and after them, had entered the realm of pure mathematics.[65]

CHAPTER FIVE

DAILY LIFE

Modern scholars have learned a great deal about the Mayan kings who left detailed records in stelae, murals, and temples constructed to honor their accomplishments. These rulers controlled the populace through religious dogma and military might, but they also built astonishing cities using human labor voluntarily provided by the average citizen. Alfredo Barrera Vásquez of the Yucatán Institute of Anthropology and History explains:

> On the one hand, you found the elite—a small group of priests and chiefs charged with preserving knowledge. They understood astronomy, architecture, engineering, art. They alone knew how to plan the building of the great monuments. They alone knew the meaning of everything in the temples. They could predict eclipses and cast horoscopes. They could decipher the history carved in the stelae and add to it. In return they led splendid lives.

> Luxury items like jade, feathers, and jaguar pelts were reserved for their exclusive use. It was the function of the rest of the population to provide these luxuries for the lords, as well as to meet all their everyday needs. So the commoners farmed, cut wood, hunted, and then bore the fruits of their labors to the ceremonial centers. When the elite traveled, it was even the duty of the people to carry them in litters [coaches] on their shoulders. [66]

While no record exists of the average Mayan citizens who supported such royal lifestyles, common people left records of their lives in household remains—cooking pots, eating utensils, and even garbage. The Mayans also left behind houses whose size, shape, and location inform archaeologists of living patterns in typical villages and cities.

To study such populations, researchers have unearthed innumerable small mounds under which Mayan houses have been buried over the centuries. Populations have also been estimated by using the number of wells, cisterns, and reservoirs in a given area. But, as Robert J. Sharer writes, "Regardless of what is counted, there is always the unknown proportion of features that have been completely destroyed or gone undetected."[67]

Despite the variables, population researchers have estimated that the Mayan

DRESS AND APPEARANCE

In *The Maya*, Spanish missionary Diego de Landa writes about the appearance and dress of the average Mayan in the sixteenth century.

"The Indians of Yucatán are a well-built people . . . robust, and very strong. . . . [Men are around five feet tall, women around four foot eight inches]. . . .

[Men] grew their hair long like women and on top of their heads they burned a space like a large tonsure [part of a monk's head that has been shaved]. . . . They braided the long part and made a wreath of it about their head leaving the queue to hang behind like a tassel.

They washed often . . . [and] were fond of sweet smells and for this reason carried bouquets of flowers and odorous herbs, which were very intricate and well-made. . . .

Their clothing consisted of a strip of cloth a hand's breadth across which served them both as breeches and stockings. They wound this several times around the waist so that one of the ends fell down in front and the other behind; and their wives carefully decorated these ends with featherwork. They wore long square cloaks which they tied to their shoulders, and sandals of hemp and dry untanned deerhide but no other clothing besides."

city with the largest population density during the late classic period was Tikal, with about ninety to one hundred thousand people within an eighty-square-mile area. The greater Copán region might have held about twenty to twenty-five thousand Mayan citizens. Of course, populations rose and fell over the several millennia that the Mayans ruled Mesoamerica. Populations peaked around A.D. 250, declined, then peaked again around 800.

An Agricultural Community

The large population densities found in Copán, Tikal, and elsewhere were a result of a successful farming culture that was able to produce food for many people. The principal crops grown by Mayan farmers were several varieties of maize (corn), beans, sweet potatoes, and squashes. The Mayans also grew cotton, for clothing, and cacao, a plant whose seeds are used to make chocolate. And just as they had assigned specific gods to the winds, sky, and days of the week, the Mayans also believed that each of their food crops was divine.

The Mayans were able to grow sufficient crops and feed themselves without the benefits of work animals, the wheel, or metal tools. Ralph Whitlock explains Mayan farming techniques:

> The preparation, sowing, and harvesting of maize was a communal effort by up to 20 men, chiefly because that was the most economical way of setting about it. First a patch of forest had to be selected and then cleared, a formidable task for men armed only with stone axes. . . .

Corn was an essential crop for the ancient Mayans.

The tool for planting was a simple dibbing-stick, its point hardened in fire. With it the Maya farmer made a hole in the soil four or five inches deep and dropped in several seeds, in the hope that at least one would grow and escape destruction by pests. With such a primitive technique, thorough clearing of the land was unnecessary [as] it was easy to plant the seeds round any awkward stumps that remained standing. Thereafter, the only tasks were to keep the land weeded as far as possible (a herculean undertaking) and to protect the crop against larger pests; some of the bigger trunks and branches were built into a stockade to keep out marauding animals, but birds were a major nuisance, and, as in every tropical country, insects took a heavy toll.[68]

The Mayans used the stalks of the maize to support bean plants that were surrounded by pumpkin, squash, and a turniplike root vegetable called sweet cassava. The edges of the fields were adorned with chili peppers, and the peppers were also grown in homes as ornamental plants. In the yards surrounding their homes, people planted pineapples and fruit trees, including papayas, avocados, and guavas.

In addition to food crops, Mayan farmers grew several plants that had a wide variety of uses. The gourd tree produced large melons that, while inedible, could be crafted into sturdy drinking cups. The stems of the hemp plant yields a strong fiber that the Mayans used for sandals, fishing line, rope, and twine. The ceiba tree, which the Mayans considered sacred, provided a fine cottonlike seed that was used in pillows. The resin of the sapodilla tree, a source of chicle for chewing gum, was boiled into strong glue that was used for multiple purposes.

The surrounding jungle provided the Mayans with many other useful products. The sap of the copal tree was burned as incense at ceremonies, and gathering copal was a profitable business. Cedar trees were cut and carved into dugout canoes, the bark of the brazilwood tree yielded a red clothing dye, and palm leaves were used for thatching roofs.

A Nutritious Diet

After harvesting their crops, the Mayans dried their beans and maize, storing the surplus. When it was time to cook with the maize, Mayan women soaked it in water and caustic powdered lime overnight so that the husk around each kernel fell off and the grain became soft and partially prepared. In addition to removing the husk, this process also released important amino acids that added nutritional value to the corn.

The maize was then ground on a grinding stone called a metate, and it was then either stored in lumps or rolled flat into tortillas. In the sixteenth century, Spanish missionary Diego de Landa wrote extensively of the Mayan diet and food preparation:

They grind [maize] between stones and, while half-ground, make large balls and [loaves] of it to give to workmen, travelers, and sailors; and these balls last several months, and only become sour [but do not go bad]. . . .

From the most finely ground maize they extract a milk which they

A modern Mayan woman rolls tortillas with a metate, a grinding stone also used by ancient Mayans.

thicken over the fire to make into a kind of porridge, which they drink hot in the morning. They throw water on what is left over from the morning and drink it during the day because they are not accustomed to drink water on its own. They also toast and grind the maize and dilute it with a little pepper and cacao, which makes a most refreshing drink.

From the ground maize and cacao they make a foaming drink with which they celebrate their feasts. They extract from cacao a grease which resembles butter, and from this and from the maize they make another drink which is both tasty and highly regarded. They make another drink from the substance of the ground maize when it is raw, which is most refreshing and tasty.

They make bread [corn tortillas] in a number of ways; and it is a good and healthy bread; but it is bad to eat when cold so the Indian women go to pains to make it twice a day. They have not succeeded in making a flour that can be kneaded like wheat flour, and if, as they sometimes do, they make bread like ours it is worthless.[69]

Black beans were another important source of nutrition for the Mayans. These were cooked and eaten whole, mashed, or refried. When combined with corn, these beans provide complete protein for a healthful diet. Squashes were cooked or dried over a fire and combined in sauces with chili peppers and other indigenous herbs and vegetables.

Although the maize and bean diet allowed people to survive without meat, a variety of wild and domestic animals provided additional protein for the Mayans. The Mayans domesticated turkeys and dogs, both of which were eaten, especially at ceremonious occasions and on holidays. In the surrounding rain forest, Mayan hunters armed with blowguns, spears, traps, and bows and arrows were able to obtain a wide variety of wild game, including deer, rabbits, wild pigs, armadillos, and monkeys. This meat was either roasted over a fire or made into a soup or stew with hot peppers and other seasonings. The Mayans also supplemented their diet with fish, snails, and shellfish from rivers, lakes, and the oceans.

The Mayan Home

The average Mayan family built a rectangular house from stone or sun-dried clay bricks known as adobe. The roofs were of pole-and-thatch construction, a combination of sturdy tree branches and dried palm fronds, rushes, and other vegetable matter. Some houses were made entirely of pole-and-thatch. Inside the ruins of Mayan homes, archaeologists have found kitchen tools, eating utensils, hearths, and the remains of food. In addition to dwelling spaces, the Mayans constructed workshops where textiles were woven, pottery was manufactured, or stone tools were produced.

The Mayans built their homes in clusters of up to six dwellings, which were called *nalil*, where extended families resided together sharing a common patio. These families might include grandparents, parents, aunts, uncles, and married children with their small children all living in separate shelters. If a family had servants or slaves, their shelters were also included in the *nalil*. Whitlock explains one aspect of the Mayan housing system:

When a man married he was expected to live near his father-in-law and to work for him for a number of years, so on his marriage a small hut was erected for him and his bride near his father-in-law's house. When the young man's term of service was over, he was helped by the community to build a larger hut to house his growing family.[70]

A DAY IN THE LIFE

In *The Ancient Sun Kingdoms of the Americas*, Victor W. von Hagen describes a typical day in the life of an average Mayan family.

"The woman rose first, between 3 and 4 A.M., rousing the flames from the smoldering ash in the *koben*, the three-stone hearth; if a household had a slave, he or she carried out this task. . . . [The woman then prepared tortillas for breakfast.]

When the Maya farmer departed in the early dawn for the fields, he took with him several apple-sized balls of ground maize wrapped in leaves. Steeped in water and flavored with burning hot chili peppers, these became his lunch, to which he added perhaps a piece of dried venison. His diet, mainly carbohydrate, was less than twenty-five hundred calories a day, yet many waxed fat on it, as Maya wall paintings and ceramics reveal. . . .

The farmer returned early in the afternoon. The women, by custom, had a hot bath ready for him. In the large centers such as Tikal and Chichén Itzá, there were communal steam baths. Where these were not available, the common man contented himself with a crudely made steam bath or hot water in an improvised tub, with a dip later in the local well.

The evening meal was the only elaborate one of the day. The menfolk sat in a circle, some on low wooden stools, the others on woven grass mats, and were served by the women. . . .

Washing preceded and followed meals. A natural detergent was used, the roots of the soapberry tree. . . .

[After dinner] the Maya man . . . sat in semidarkness and worked wood, jade, or cotton into articles of trade, or made weapons. His wife spun cotton and wove mantas [rough-textured cotton cloth]. In the highlands they made light with pine splinters, as bright as candles."

A modern Mayan woman prepares a chicken dinner.

Mayan families lived in rectangular houses built from stone or sun-dried clay that were covered with pole-and-thatch roofs.

According to Mayan custom, when a family member died, he or she was buried beneath the floor of the home. The house was then abandoned and used as a religious shrine where the dead relative was venerated.

Mayan people were known for welcoming visitors into their homes. According to de Landa,

> The people of Yucatán are very generous and hospitable, for no one enters their homes without him being given whatever food and drink they ~ay have. During the daytime they ~rinks and in the evening food, ~y do not have it themselves,

they go out and ask for it in the neighborhood. And if travelers join them on the roads, they must give something to everyone they meet, although they themselves are thereby left with much less.[71]

Family and Children

The Mayan family found happiness in life based on a repetitive cycle of tradition and religious beliefs, centered on the 260-day sacred almanac that was believed to track their destinies from birth to death. Just as some people in modern times use astrology to determine their futures, the Maya relied heavily on the calendar to answer questions about their fates and those of their children. As Sharer writes, "The date of each person's birth in the 260-day almanac had different attributes—some good, some neutral, some bad. In this way each person's birth date controlled his or her temperament and destiny."[72]

Even before a Mayan woman became pregnant, supernatural deities were called to intervene. In the Yucatán region, Mayan women traveled to the island of Cozumel to ask Ix Chel, the goddess of childbirth, to help them conceive. This journey, according to Victor W. von Hagen, involved "a hazardous twenty-mile trip in an open dugout canoe across the wind-whipped channel separating it from the Yucatán mainland."[73] If a woman could not make the journey, she instead put a doll with the image of Ix Chel under her bed.

Once a child was born, it was named after his or her date of birth. As scholar Alfredo Barrera Väsquez explains,

> In his lifetime a Maya bore three names. Say he was born on the date 7 Ahau of the Maya calendar. His name until puberty would be simply Seven Ahau. When he was initiated into manhood, he would assume a new name that reflected some personal feature. Say he was short. Then he would be known as Tzap, or Short One. Not until he was married did he assume his formal name. Supposing his mother came from the Poot family and his father was an Uuc, his adult name would be Na Poot Uuc, literally an Uuc born of a mother [Na] named Poot.

An ultimate refinement was also possible. The name of a man's profession, or some noteworthy characteristic, might replace his mother's name. If our hypothetical child had proved very courageous in battle, he might have been known as Ah Dziik Uuc, or the Uuc Brave One.[74]

The Mayans did not send their children to formal schools, but children were trained for specialized roles from an early age. Average boys also learned from their fathers to farm, fish, and hunt. Girls, on the other hand, were trained by their mothers to cook, sew, weave, make pottery, and barter at the local markets.

Building a Society

The Mayans sometimes used cacao beans or stone beads as money, but when it came to taxes, average citizens were called on by kings and nobility to contribute in a number of ways. Mayan farmers turned a portion of their surplus maize over to tax collectors, who placed it in a state-owned storage facility to be used to feed the upper classes. In addition, citizens were called on to work for free in the maize, cotton, and chili pepper fields owned by priests and nobles. The artists who carved the facades, lintels, and stelae, and decorated Mayan buildings were also supported by these volunteer farmhands.

The ruling classes benefited in other ways—most notably, their homes were built and paid for by average citizens. The wide causeways between palaces and temples were also built by citizen-laborers, as were reservoirs, ball courts, and other public facilities. T. Patrick Culbert writes about the construction of the beautiful Mayan cities:

> What makes Maya sites so impressive is their wonderful stone buildings. The labor invested in their

Citizen-laborers built many ancient Mayan structures, including this ball court at Copán.

construction is beyond comprehension. Crowds of humble peasants must have quarried stone from the limestone bedrock, then carried it to construction sites; others, meanwhile, amassed piles of wood to feed the fires that transformed limestone into mortar and plaster. Then there must have been hordes of more specialized workers: masons, plasterers, carvers (at sites with decorated facades), as well as architects to design it all.[75]

These workers, however, were not slaves. As von Hagen writes, "The [average citizen] could always be counted on to work willingly in the construction of a temple-city, since in the long run it would benefit him. All wished to gain favor with the gods."[76]

Weaving a Legacy

Whereas men worked as farmers and builders, Mayan women were known as skilled weavers, basket makers, and feather workers. Weaving was an activity that was practiced on an almost continuous basis. De Landa writes that Mayan women "have the custom of helping each other weave cloth, and they take the same pleasure in these labors as their husbands do in working on the land, and during work they always have their mocking jokes and tell each other news and sometimes they gossip a little."[77]

FEATHER MOSAICS

Mayan women wove bird plumage into incredible works of art, known as feather mosaics, which were used for a variety of purposes. The weaver laid out the feathers into specific patterns and wove the quill into the nap of a cloth.

Men's breechcloths were decorated with these colorful mosaics, as were the ornamental helmets worn by priests. During ceremonies, dancers used feather mosaics in costumes and banners while kings were cooled by feather fans employed by servants.

The brightest and most beautiful feathers were considered the most valuable items in Mayan society. In *The Ancient Sun Kingdoms of the Americas* Victor W. von Hagen lists some of the birds used by Mayan women.

"In Yucatán there was the motmot . . . with its iridescent tail, and the blue Yucatán jay . . . which traveled in flocks and yielded a wide variety of blue plumes. There were the modest-plumed quail, woodpeckers, pheasants, and the yellow-crested curassow, whose blue-black feathers were made into a feather mosaic for high priests. The ocellated wild turkey [having an eyelike colored spot on its feathers] gave feathers which were used in Maya rituals. Along the seashore were ducks, egrets, herons, and the sun bittern. In the tropical area of El Petén there were toucanets, parrots, and trogons, and farther up, in the high, cold forests of Guatemala, were the long-tailed green and red parrots and the fabled quetzal . . . which yielded two long, golden green tail feathers. The quetzal lives in the highlands and breeds in the cloud forests, above 4,000 feet. [As Diego de Landa writes,] 'In the province of Verapaz [in Guatemala] they punish with death he who kills the quetzal bird, the one of the rich plumes . . . for these feathers were of great value.'"

The plumage of the quetzal was prized by ancient Mayan weavers.

After the cotton thread was spun on a simple spindle, it was colored with vegetable and mineral dye. Each color had a specific symbolic meaning, as described by von Hagen:

Black was the symbol of war, since [a warrior used an] obsidian tipped arrow and spear. . . . Yellow, the color of ripe corn, was the symbol for food. . . . Red was a blood symbol. . . . Cochineal [red dye made of the dried and pulverized bodies of cochineal insects] was highly prized. . . . It was obtained from the insects that Maya boys [according to de Landa] "herded like cows" on cactus pads. . . .

The Mayas . . . made [dyes] from the wild tomato, the blackberry, and the green-black avocado. The most prized, because it was difficult to obtain, was the deep purple obtained from a mollusk. . . . Dyes were pounded in stone mortars, which are sometimes found in graves. The dry colors were doubtless kept in small bags.[78]

Mayan women wove the dyed thread into beautiful cloth. In addition, they used yarn woven from rabbit wool and brightly colored feathers woven into mosaics.

Women also used their weaving skills to construct baskets from reeds, grass, rushes, vines, and other materials. Woven rush mats were also essential items in Mayan households and were used as flooring, mattresses, and to hold food.

Life Portrayed in Clay

Mayan women were potters as well as weavers, and they created some of the highest quality

Ancient Mayan pottery ranks with the world's best.

pottery found anywhere in the world. Women did not use potter's wheels but instead laid long round coils of clay in successive rings. The finished pots were smoothed with a broken piece of pottery called a shard, then fired in a wood-, charcoal-, or grass-fired kiln.

Everyone from the humblest peasant to the mightiest king used pottery, and pots were mass-produced using molds to press standardized patterns into the clay before baking. Clay was formed into plates, cups, vases, and pitchers. Clay stoves, called braziers, were used to burn incense and heat homes. Jars five feet high were used to store water, and delicately decorated urns held the cremated remains of nobles.

Additionally, clay idols—replicas of deities—were formed, some standing as tall as an average person. As von Hagen explains,

Decorated with scenes of Maya life, the most beautiful pottery was made for the dead. The . . . clay figures . . . were freely molded yet exquisite in detail, showing Maya chieftains elegantly dressed and women richly clothed with necklaces and elaborate coiffures. . . . Their pottery has left us many details of Maya life, especially the life of the women, which is [rarely] indicated in the carvings on monuments.[79]

Trading at Mayan Markets

The creative output of the Mayan people was on display in every city, town, and village at centralized markets where goods were sold and bartered on a weekly basis. Mesoamerica was crossed by hundreds of miles of well-constructed roads that were detailed on maps painted on fine cloth. Goods transported via these roads were carried on the backs of porters in long, winding human caravans through the jungles. Other goods were packed into dugout canoes and were transported along river and sea routes.

The markets were divided into sections, one area specializing in merchants who sold food, another clothing, and yet another pottery. Merchants squatted beneath cotton awnings and offered, according to von Hagen, "salt, dried fish, cotton yardage, copal, honey, wax, corn, beans, and feathers woven into cloaks, shields, and caps. Certain tribes of the Mayas had a virtual monopoly on salt." Luxury items might include, "cacao, stone beads, green stones called *tuns* . . . nose beads, cochineal for dyeing, alum . . . [pelts] of jaguar and puma, fruits, vanilla beans (to season the chocolate), wood, lime, and clay."[80]

Hundreds of other items might also be found at a typical Mayan market, including jadeite from the northern highlands, obsidian and hematite from the southern highlands, tobacco from the lowlands, amber from Chiapas in southern Mexico, and shark teeth, shells, coral, stingray spines, and tortoise shells from coastal regions.

Human slaves, as well as material goods, were always for sale at Mayan markets. As Whitlock writes,

> Slaves were required to do much of the hard manual work of well-to-do households. They carried merchandise on their backs, paddled canoes, fanned flies away from their exalted masters, collected the noxious materials used for dyeing, and ground maize meal. The market price of an adult, able-bodied slave [in the sixteenth century] was . . . 100 cocoabeans. Slaves were, it seems, not badly treated, but when an important person died his slaves were often knocked on the head and buried with him. They were also frequently pressed into service as a sacrifice to this god or that, unless the need for divine favours was desperate enough to call for the offering of a free man.[81]

While individual merchants bartered for the best deals at the outdoor markets, wholesale importers occupied stone warehouses full of cargo from near and far. These traders argued over terms of credit, payment methods, and delivery dates, sealing each deal with an alcoholic drink of pulque. If a merchant failed to pay or delivered shoddy goods, he might find himself at war with his customers.

The market, held about every five days, attracted many people to the temples and plazas of such large cities as Tikal and Copán—places that were otherwise deserted

Ancient Mayan markets attracted many customers to the large cities, including Tikal (pictured) and Copán.

except during ceremonial events. Whitlock explains that, during the carnival-like atmosphere of the market, the city would come alive:

> Buyers and sellers, [when] their business [was] done, would come to gaze and make offerings at humbler shrines; persons of rank, borne in litters, would worship secludedly at the great shrines or gather for a council of state; a game of ball would be going on with many onlookers crowding to see the play; and perhaps dancers decked in fantastic masks

would weave their patterns on some sunlit court to the sound of drum and flute.[82]

Music and Dance

Most aspects of Mayan religious and ceremonial life were accompanied by music and dancing, and drums, flutes, and percussion were the driving forces behind the music. This is illustrated in the heir-ascension mural at Bonampak, which shows a ceremonial procession led by nine musicians, some of whom are shaking gourd rattles while others beat out the rhythm on turtle shells and a wooden drum.

The Mayans played several types of drums, large and small. Some were carried; others rested on the ground. Drums were made of hollowed-out logs decorated with beautiful designs and covered with a deerskin head. The Mayans also used pottery to make ceramic drums. De Landa describes several Mayan drums and trumpets:

> They have small drums which they play with the hand and another kind of drum made of hollow wood which has a heavy sad sound and which they beat with a rather long stick which is padded with the gum from a tree around the end. They have long thin trumpets made of hollow wood with large twisted gourds at the end. They also have another instrument made from a whole tortoise together with its shell but with the flesh removed; and this is beaten with the palm of the hand, producing a sad, lugubrious [mournful] sound.
>
> They have whistles which are made from the leg bones of deer and from large shells and also reed flutes, and with these instruments they made music for the dancers.[83]

In addition to the trumpet described by de Landa, Mayan musicians played large conch shells, whose bellowing blasts were used to call down the gods. Five-foot-long trumpets made with wood and clay were always blown two at a time, each horn having a different harmonious note. Flutes were made from deer bones, reeds, clay, or even human leg bones. The pan pipe, consisting of five reeds joined together each with a dif-ferent note, is still popular in Mesoamerica and elsewhere.

Percussive instruments were played by dancers as well as musicians. Dancers tied bells on their wrists, ankles, and waists and played rattles made from bone, gourds, and shells. Dancers also sang, clapped hands, and stomped their feet for rhythmic effect.

Dancing was done for religious ceremonial purposes such as celebrating holidays or before going to war. These dances were often based on the movements of animals. One such dance, performed by two haggard men in the underworld, is described in the *Popol*

A modern Mayan playing a hollow log drum carries on the musical tradition of his ancestors.

Vuh: "They . . . performed the dance of the *puhuy* [owl or churn owl], the dance of the *cux* [weasel], and the dance of the *iboy* [armadillo], and they also danced the *xtzul* [centipede] and the *chitic* [a dance performed on very tall stilts]."[84]

De Landa describes two dances he witnessed:

> They have in particular two dances which are well worth seeing. One is danced with sticks, so they call it *colomche*, which has that meaning. To dance it, a great circle of dancers gathers to the sound of Indian music, which sets the pace for them, and then two of them leave the circle in time to the rhythm. One of these dancers clutches a handful of sticks and dances upright with them, the other dances squatting on his heels. Both move in time with the circle, and the one with the sticks throws them with all his strength at the other who, with great skill, catches them with a small stick. When they have finished throwing they return in rhythm to the circle while others leave to do the same as they have done. There is another dance in which some eight hundred Indians dance with small flags and long war-like steps to music and not one of them is out of time. These dances are very tiring because they do not stop all day long and the dancers are given food and drink there. It is not customary for the men to dance with the women.[85]

The music and dance of the ancient Mayans are reminders that the average citizen was often entertained in a rich and interesting manner. During the classic period, food was in abundance, trade brought a wide variety of goods to the Mayans, and dozens of yearly ceremonies and ball games amused the populace. In times of peace the Mayans lived in communities where cooperation, spirituality, and generosity were a part of daily life.

CHAPTER SIX

THE DECLINE AND FALL OF MAYAN CIVILIZATION

The majesty of Mayan power began to shrink around the ninth century, during an era researchers call the terminal classic period. During this time Copán collapsed in 822 and Tikal fell in 869, dates determined by the last inscriptions at each site. While the people in those cities did not completely vanish on those dates, the lack of further inscriptions is indicative of a breakdown of religious authority and government hierarchy.

Other Mayan cities suffered similar fates in the late classic period. Since each city was autonomous, they each rose and fell independent from one another—often for unexplainable reasons. As Ralph Whitlock writes, "The Maya cities . . . grew like spring flowers, enjoyed their summer of glory, and then either experienced a natural decline into . . . old age or were slashed [by enemies] into oblivion."[86]

During the terminal classic period, archaeological records in central and southern lowland sites show a halt in construction of temples, palaces, monuments, and ceremonial and administrative buildings. Manufacturing appears to have stopped, as ritual items made from pottery, jade, shell, and other materials vanished. Researchers have concluded that this demonstrates that the ruling elite who directed and oversaw production of these items either lost power or perished. In *Maya: The Riddle and Rediscovery of a Lost Civilization*, respected Mayan scholar Charles Gallenkamp dramatically describes the inexplicable decline:

> Intellectual pursuits ground to a halt; the elaborate ritualism which had nourished the growth of Mayan culture was seemingly abandoned. Even the computation of time—the guidepost against which all acts and events had been measured—ceased to be important. Incredible though it may seem, the Maya evacuated their long-cherished places of worship, leaving the labor of centuries to the ravages of time.

> The temples were emptied of their priestly guardians, copal incense no longer smoldered upon sacred altars within them, voices had ceased to echo from the plazas. Yet the cities were left untouched, without destruction or alteration, as if their inhabitants had expected to return

Inscriptions discovered at the site of Tikal indicate that the ancient city fell in 869.

momentarily. But they did not. Instead, an immense stillness enveloped them from which they were never again to awaken. Grass overtook the courtyards, vines and the spreading roots of trees crept into doorways and sought nourishment in the lime mortar between the stones of pyramids and temples, forcing them to part and crumble. Within a century the jungle had reclaimed the ill-destined cities of the Maya. That an energetic empire should have been totally forsaken at the very height of its glory is a phenomenon without historical parallel.[87]

While sites such as Tikal and Copán fell to ruin, power shifted north to Yucatán cities such as Chichén Itzá, which was growing rapidly. But even as the northern lowlands achieved greater power, there was, according to Robert J. Sharer, "profound political change. Long-count dates, for so long used to chronicle the achievements of the supreme rulers . . . were no longer being recorded in the north *or* in the south."[88]

The Fall of Copán

Copán, the southernmost city in the Mayan region, was a major power center from approximately A.D. 460 to 800. One of the more astounding features that archaeologists discovered at Copán was the sixty-three-step Hieroglyphics Stairway, which is inscribed with over twenty-two hundred glyphs, the longest such inscription in Copán's history. This monumental task was dedicated in 756, indicating that Copán was still a powerful city-state at that time. Nine years later, in 765, glyphs indicated that priests from all over Mesoamerica met in Copán to correct minor errors in the calendar, indicating that the city was still an important center for scholarly research.

There is little doubt that Copán was a major urban center. Archaeologists have found that a 9.25-square-mile section of the Copán valley contains over thirty-five hundred mounds that are the overgrown ruins of buildings. Thousands more lie up and down the valley from this main group.

Despite Copán's place among the great Mayan cities, the people of the region slowly left the area in the ninth century and eventually abandoned it completely. It was the fate of Yax Pac, who rose to the throne in 763, to be Copán's last ruler honored in stone. His hold on the government's central authority was greatly diminished from that of his predecessors, and in its place, lesser nobles gained greater power. Sharer writes of the events that led to Yax Pac's downfall:

As Yax Pac tried to keep the kingdom together by rewarding his officials with more titles and greater status, he

The ruins of the ancient city of Copán, a major urban center until its decline in the ninth century.

A City's Violent Collapse

In 1989 Arthur A. Demarest, a professor of anthropology at Vanderbilt University and the director of the Petexbatún Archaeological Project, supervised a team of forty scientists and over one hundred laborers to uncover the mystery of the Mayan collapse. Demarest's work took him to Dos Pilas, a capital founded in 645 by a prince from Tikal, known by researchers simply as Ruler Four, who conquered a region that encompassed 1,500 square miles of surrounding territory. Unlike the long, slow collapse of the Copán civilization, the story of Ruler Four illustrates a sudden, violent end to one of the great Mayan cities. Demarest wrote about his discoveries in the February 1993 issue of *National Geographic.*

"In 761 something went wrong. According to hieroglyphs we deciphered, the kings of Petexbatún had overextended their domain. There had been hints of trouble for more than a decade. Ruler 4 had spent much of his 20-year reign racing from one end of the realm to the other, performing bloodletting rituals, leading battles, and contracting alliances. He used every technique to sustain the kingdom, but to no avail.

Then the city of Tamarindito threw off the yoke of Dos Pilas. . . . Warriors attacked the capital and killed Ruler 4.

We know that about that time the citizens of Dos Pilas made a valiant last stand. In desperation they ripped stones from the facades of the temples and monuments. . . . They tore down much of the royal palace to build two walls topped with wooden palisades around the central palaces and temples. We believe the warriors stood behind the inner wall, using the space between the two walls as a killing alley.

In the main plaza the remaining few hundred people crowded into a village of crude huts in the shadow of temples from the earlier epoch of grandeur. . . .

But eventually they stopped building houses and making pottery. Sometime in the early ninth century . . . [they] disappeared."

unwittingly increased the power of the nobles. They proclaimed their power on the carved thrones in their palaces, where they held court like lesser versions of the Copán king himself.

In 810 the ceremonies marking the auspicious katun ending were not held at Copán but rather at [nearby] Quirigua, where Yax Pac visited the new Quirigua ruler, Jade Sky. The end of dynastic rule at Copán is told on its last dated monument [in 822 at what researchers have labeled] Altar L . . . showing Yax Pac seated opposite a noble named U Cit Tok, who attempted to be the 17th ruler of Copán. Altar L was never finished and its inscription was never carved. U Cit Tok failed to rule Copán, and the last remnant of centralized authority vested in the king disappeared. Thereafter, power at Copán was divided among the principal nobles who lived in compounds throughout the valley.[89]

The strong central ruling authority was gone from Copán, and with it the construction of royal monuments. Other changes began to affect the Copán region as well, and the city appears to have become a victim of its own success. As the center of a prosperous kingdom, the population of Copán grew too large for the surrounding forest to support. The accompanying environmental degradation and deforestation may have played a role in the city's decline.

Scholars believe that this decline was a long process and that the Copán valley was not completely abandoned until around 1100, nearly three centuries after the rule of Yax Pac. Unlike other cities, which were destroyed by war or royal conflict, Copán's loss of power was slow and steady rather than quick and violent.

In the eighth century, the centralized government and religious hierarchy was weakened. Copán's government then collapsed completely in the ninth century. For several centuries people continued to live in the Copán valley but were ruled by small regional governors. Finally the valley was emptied out entirely as the people in the region slowly drifted off to other, more prosperous areas.

The Decline of Tikal

People had been living in the Tikal region since at least 600 B.C., and by the second century B.C. they had built majestic plazas, temples, and other buildings. Over the centuries thousands of complex architectural wonders were constructed in the Tikal region. By A.D. 200, Tikal was a city supported by trade and had become one of the major ceremonial centers in Mesoamerica. By the eighth century the city covered fifty square miles and the greater Tikal region was populated by an estimated forty thousand people.

Then, mysteriously in 889, the last stela was set in the Great Plaza, and a culture that had endured for over one thousand years suddenly disappeared. Tikal's downfall was marked by the end of temple construction and a sharp drop-off in population.

Even before Tikal was deserted, an intricately carved monument, known as Stela Twenty-Six, was vandalized and turned upside-down in a pile of rubble. Researchers believe that this sacrilegious act indicates widespread discontent with kings and priests

The jungles began to encroach on the crumbling temples and palaces of Tikal by 900.

and possibly a violent revolution against government authority.

Whatever the answer to this mystery, by the end of the 800s, squatters had moved into the once-grandiose plazas of Tikal. By 900, as the great temples and palaces crumbled and the jungle began to reclaim the land, Tikal was deserted.

Searching for Answers

The exact reasons for the collapse of Tikal, along with other Mayan cities at the time, remains a heated topic of debate among Mayan scholars. While archaeologists have dug for clues in ruins, climatologists have studied weather patterns, and environmental scientists have looked into ecological factors. Most experts agree that some sort of natural disaster, in combination with a major armed conflict or revolution, brought about the end of one of Earth's most ad-

vanced ancient societies. Each theory has its supporters as well as its detractors. The hurricane theory put forth by Sharer shows this contradiction.

The Mesoamerican region experiences several types of natural disasters, including destructive earthquakes and hurricanes. Sharer writes that "a major [hurricane] can easily destroy agricultural production over a wide area. Still, the idea that the transient and relatively localized effects of hurricanes could trigger the failure of a whole civilization is hard to swallow."[90]

Others propose that the Mayans farmed the same plots of land for so many years that the soil became depleted, producing smaller annual yields of maize and beans until the land had to be abandoned completely. These problems might have been further aggravated by a hurricane or short-term climate change as mentioned by Sharer.

The most widely accepted theories of Mayan collapse are based on a combination of natural and human-created disasters. As Sharer states,

> The idea of a revolt has been extremely popular. Several investigators have suggested that the increasing size of the ruling class, combined with its abuses of power, led to a popular revolt. . . . The thesis holds that a combination of factors, including agricultural difficulties, malnutrition or disease, and perhaps even natural disasters—all bespeaking a chronic failure of the elite to intercede with the gods—culminated in a widespread disillusionment among the Maya peasant class and a loss of confidence in the rulers. . . . The proposed result was a violent revolt by the peasants and the destruction of the ruling class. [91]

A more fascinating factor might have intensified the Mayan decline: The Mayans were strong believers in the predictions of their calendars. Each round of thirteen *katuns*, or 256-year cycles, had its own set of predictions and prophecies. Some scholars believe that new *katun* that began in 790 was associated with the end of Mayan prosperity. As a self-fulfilling prophesy, Sharer writes,

> the fatalistic Mayans may have failed to resist the [negative] forces of change that were sweeping away the old order out of a conviction that it would be futile to challenge prophecies that foretold fundamental changes in their society—particularly

when the signs of decline were already there for all to see. [92]

Economic factors also might have played a role in the downfall of the southern lowland powers. Some researchers suggest that the trade that kept the cities of Tikal and Copán connected to the coastal and northern regions might have broken down, leaving the former trade centers economically isolated.

Hostile outside forces may have had an influence, according to this theory. While the Mayans dominated Mesoamerica for many centuries, there were other cultures on the edges of the Mayan realm. A group known as the Putun Mayans, who resided in the present-day Mexican state of Tabasco on the Gulf Coast, were not part of the Mayan social and religious heritage. The Putuns, also known as the Itza, were not a single culture but a loosely knit group who shared a common language known as Chontal. Sharer explains:

> The Putun Maya were both warriors and merchants, and their aggressive undertakings during the Postclassic seem to have been motivated by a desire to seize and control important resources and trade routes. Initially, they seemed to have been concerned with maintaining several old riverine and overland routes in the central and southern lowland that had flourished during the Classic period. Eventually, however, they came to control the seacoast trade around the Yucatán Peninsula, which connected the east and west coasts, and, ultimately, the commerce between Gulf-coast Mexico and Central America. [93]

According to this theory, when the Putuns took control of the trade routes leading to and from the southern lowland capitals, the economic resources of the cities dried up and people were forced to move to cities with better trade prospects.

The Rise and Fall of Chichén Itzá

Whatever caused the downfall of the southern lowland region of the Mayan realm, the Putuns played an important part in continuing the culture in a different region. Researchers refer to the Putun culture as "Mexicanized," meaning they added central Mexican influence to Mayan art, pottery, architecture, government, religion, and other cultural traits.

The power of the Mayans certainly did shift north to the Yucatán Peninsula in present-day Mexico when the terminal classic period ended and the postclassic began. But, according to *The Magnificent Maya*,

as researchers . . . developed a more sophisticated understanding of the culture's architectural trends, and broadened their archaeological knowledge of the region, it became increasingly apparent that there was no clear-cut division between south and north or between old and new. . . . Evidence showed that several Yucatán cities were occupied well before the collapse of the great centers in Guatemala and Honduras.[94]

While the southern cities were in decline, power definitely shifted to the north in the tenth century. In this new era about seven large Yucatán cities, including Chichén Itzá, Cobá, Mayapán, and Uxmal, became political,

economic, and religious centers of Mayan culture. And these cities were built close together, some within fifteen miles of each other.

Also around the tenth century, the Putun Mayans developed large seagoing canoes that allowed them to dominate the trade in the Yucatán region. As the importance of trade on the peninsula grew, people began to move there from other regions. And, according to Sharer, the Putuns "established new coastal trading centers. . . . [And] with the founding of a new . . . political and religious capital [in Chichén Itzá], the Putun Maya opened a new era in the history of Maya civilization, an era that—more than any other—had far reaching consequences throughout Mesoamerica."[95]

The Temple of Warriors was one of the eleventh-century construction projects in Chichén Itzá.

THE WELL OF SACRIFICE

Chichén Itzá is named after the three large wells, or cenotes that lay outside the city. In Mayan, *chi* means "mouth," and *chen* means "well." Thus *Chichén Itzá* means "the Mouth of the Well of the Itzá." One well, referred to as the Sacred Cenote or the Well of Sacrifice, has aroused particular interest among researchers. The murky green water of the Sacred Cenote lies in a hole two hundred feet across and sixty-five feet below the surface in a natural limestone pit.

In 1843, explorer John Lloyd Stephens described the well in *Incidents of Travel in Yucatán*: "A mysterious influence seemed to pervade it, in unison with the historical account that the well of Chichen was a place of pilgrimage, and that the human victims were thrown into it in sacrifice." In addition to humans, the Mayans made offerings to the well of precious stones, art objects, and gold.

Other explorers would find fascination with the Sacred Cenote. In 1894 American explorer Edward Thompson bought a hacienda whose lands contained the Sacred Cenote. After studying the well for ten years, Thompson built a derrick on the rim of the cliff and four native workmen began dredging the thirty-five-foot-deep silt at the bottom of the water.

After a week of pulling up dead leaves, brown muck, broken branches, and other debris, the workers found a human finger bone, then pieces of pottery, jade, copal resin, and artifacts such as cooking tools, obsidian knives, and spears. Soon the well was giving up skulls and bones. Eventually forty-two different individuals—men, women, and children between ten and twelve years old—were pulled from the Sacred Cenote. Although it had been rumored for centuries, that the Sacred Cenote was used for human sacrifice, Thompson's discoveries proved that the Well of Sacrifice was indeed appropriately named.

During the century that followed, Chichén Itzá became the site of dozens of major construction projects, including El Castillo, the Caracol Observatory, and the imposing Temple of Warriors, surrounded by two hundred carved columns.

Although the southern Mayans were known for their battles and human sacri-fice, the new Mayan rulers were even fiercer in their military and religious practices. Murals, sculptures, and other artwork from this period focus on war, torture of prisoners, and human sacrifice as never before. This new cultural imposition, however, was not appreciated by the native Mayans. In *The Book of the Jaguar Priest*, it is written, "[For] the present we must carry . . . the sons of Itza on our backs, maintaining them in our midst, like a great stone of misfortune."[96]

This fierce new attitude was also noted at what is undoubtedly the most famous of the thirteen ball courts in Chichén Itzá. Located at the Temple of the Jaguars, the Great Ball Court measures 274 feet by 120 feet and is marked by rings 4 feet in diameter and 20 feet off the ground. The object of the Mayan ball game was to hit a ball with the elbows, wrists, or hips—but without the use of the hands or feet—through the hole in the ring that measured 19 inches across. This was so difficult a task that when it occurred, the game was over. As Sharer explains, the mural carved into the Great Ball

Court's walls relate to the deadly seriousness of this game:

The relief sculptures . . . depict a . . . gruesome outcome [of] at least one version of the ballgame that was played here—the ritual reenactment of warfare culminating in the sacrifice of captives. On the left stands an apparently victorious ballplayer or warrior with a knife in one hand and the head of his vanquished foe in the other. The decapitated foe, with streams of blood transformed into serpents spurting from his neck, kneels to the right of a disk, or shield, bearing a death's head [a human skull representing death].[97]

Ancient Mayan ball players were only permitted to strike the ball with their elbows, wrists, or hips.

DEADLY BALL GAMES

The Mayans took their ball games very seriously. Winning players were honored with riches as great as modern sports heroes. Losers were decapitated. In *The Cities of Ancient Mexico*, Jeremy A. Sabloff takes readers to the scene of a Mayan ball game in Uxmal circa A.D. 900.

"The players take their places at opposite ends of the court. . . . The large hard ball, made from the sap of a rubber tree, is produced. The object of the game is to hit the ball through the rings, carved with hieroglyphic inscriptions, that are set high in the vertical walls forming the two . . . sides of the court. Each team aims for one of the rings. . . . The ball must be hit by a player's body and not by his hands or feet. The game is over when one team hits the ball through the ring—either directly or by bouncing it off the wall. . . . This is no sporting event but a contest of great religious and political significance with the opposing teams representing different religious forces.

After many attempts at hitting the ball through the rings . . . the player sees his opportunity and shoots a glorious, well-angled shot from his hip . . . and the game is over. Uxmal and its gods have triumphed over the forces of Kabah and the gods of the underworld.

As leader of the winning team the player is presented with fine jewelry, including a necklace of jade beads. The . . . leader of the losing team is dragged forward. His playing equipment is pulled from his body roughly, and he is bound head and foot by ropes. Slumped in shame, he is carried . . . back to the main temple. There he will be decapitated by the high priest . . . and his body rolled down the long steps to the plaza floor below."

The End of the Ancient Mayans

By the eleventh century Chichén Itzá was one of the largest and most powerful cities in Mayan history. Then, around 1200, the city's power collapsed as mysteriously as Tikal's and Copán's had in the earlier years. Cities such as Uxmal, Kabah, Sayil, and Labná were abandoned. As Gallenkamp writes, "Elsewhere a few religious centers were kept alive by struggling priesthood. . . . The Mayan populace had not found it possible to recover from the mysterious weakness which had brought about the collapse of their age-old traditions and deprived them of their intellectual gifts."[98]

Around this time, Mayapán, less than one hundred miles to the east of Chichén Itzá, rose

The Aztecs, shown here participating in a human sacrifice ritual, rose to power after the desertion of Mayapán.

up to become a central Mayan power. Unlike other Mayan cities, which, according to *The Magnificent Maya*, "followed an orderly design in the tradition of the early Maya centers . . . Mayapán was a more shoddily constructed, walled town with a chaotic plan—a tangle of buildings of various sizes linked by narrow al-leys. The great temples that were at the core of other Maya cities were largely absent."[99]

The power of Mayapán, with a population of about twelve thousand, probably peaked in the fourteenth and fifteenth centuries. Archaeologists believe that, like several other Mayan cities before it, Mayapán was destroyed in a bloody battle, this one taking place in 1441. The city was sacked and burned as the result of a corrupt ruler named Cocom, who was overthrown by nobles known as Xiuis, after the name of their leader, Tutuxiu. Spanish bishop Diego de Landa reported on this 120 years after the city was abandoned:

> Cocom . . . introduced more Mexicans into the city, and began to tyrannize and make slaves of the common people. For this reason the lords joined forces with Tutuxiu, who was a great statesman . . . and they agreed to kill Cocom. This they did and they also killed all of his sons except for one who was away, sacked his house and seized his plantations of cacao and other fruit, saying that by so doing they were being paid for what he had taken from them. The disputes between the Cocoms, who claimed to have been driven out unjustly, and the Xiuis, lasted so long that after having been in that city for more than five hundred years, they deserted and abandoned it and each returned to his own country. [100]

Archaeologists have unearthed burned ceiling timbers and blackened pottery shards that add credence to de Landa's story.

The desertion of Mayapán marked the end of the most powerful civilization in Mesoamerica. By this time, the Aztec tribe had risen from obscurity and had consolidated their power into a magnificent empire based in present-day Mexico City. The Aztec power to the north attracted people from around the region, and the former realm dominated by Mayapán dissolved into sixteen small, bickering city-states whose armies remained perpetually at war with one another. According to *The Magnificent Maya*, "towns were continually raided for young men who were drafted as soldiers or dispatched forthwith as sacrificial victims, and fields were burned to starve villagers into submission. Art and architecture declined amid the constant skirmishing."[101] In 1464 a fierce hurricane swept through the region, further destroying any remnants of the ancient Mayan culture.

The Arrival of the Spanish

In 1511—seventy years after Mayapán was abandoned—the first Spanish explorers landed in Yucatán. The Spanish inadvertently brought the smallpox virus to Mexican shores, and the Mayans had virtually no resistance to this scourge. In 1515 a smallpox epidemic swept through the Mayan realm, killing tens of thousands of people.

The Spanish began a conquest of Central America that was to last for centuries. They were searching for gold, however, and found very little of it on the Yucatán Peninsula. It was not until 1527 that the official conquest of the Mayan lands was undertaken by 380 men under the direction of Francisco de Montejo. The Mayans were fierce warriors, and despite years of deadly warfare, they were able to keep the conquistadors at bay until 1546, when, according to Victor W. von Hagen, the Spanish "put down with terrible and indiscriminate slaughter those Maya tribes who refused the yoke of peace, and the conquest was over."[102] Over twenty centuries of Mayan cultural dominance of Mesoamerica had come to an end.

A Living Tradition

Although the Mayan culture of the distant past was lost, the Mayan people themselves have survived into the twenty-first century. These distant descendants of kings such as Smoke-Jaguar, Blue-Quetzal-Macaw, and Eighteen Rabbit continue to blend ancient tradition with newer cultural and religious practices introduced by the Spanish. Archaeologist T. Patrick Culbert comments on the Mayans today:

> The descendants of [the] ancient Maya continue to live in the northern

Descendants of the ancient Mayans continue to speak the Mayan language and wear traditional costumes.

sections of the Yucatán Peninsula and in the mountainous areas of Guatemala, Belize, and the Mexican state of Chiapas. Although the structure of ancient Maya society was destroyed by the Spaniards, the Maya of today— village people, supporting themselves mainly by age-old farming systems— continue to speak Maya languages and dress daily in traditional costumes. At ceremonies, the flute and drum sound, incense from the copal tree fills the air, and the names of the ancient gods are chanted (although nowadays intermingled with those of Christian saints). Like ethnic minorities elsewhere around the world, the Maya are under pressure from the dominant culture in their area; still on the margin of the economic and political systems of Mexico and Guatemala, they must struggle to maintain their lands and customs. But the Maya have faced difficult times before, and they have survived.[103]

In the early years of the twenty-first century, the lands where the ancient Mayans live are experiencing an unprecedented population boom. Regions that were once nearly inaccessible are now filled with growing numbers of impoverished people who, for their basic survival, are forced to cut down the forests, graze cattle, and hunt local animals into extinction. In 1993 Culbert wrote about this situation and how it impacts the study of Mayan archaeology:

> While a significant thrill of Maya archaeology has always been the ex-

citement of exploring a forested area without the aid of roads or maps, the days of such excitement are numbered. As recently as my own early days with the Tikal Project in the 1960s, nothing but forest covered the 18-mile stretch northward from Lake Peten Itza (where the only sizable modern population lived) to Tikal. Today [1993], this forest is gone; farmsteads line a road that did not exist 30 years ago. And the colonists continue to arrive, mostly peasant farmers from land-poor sections of Guatemala. At present there remain vast areas of unoccupied forest north of Tikal. Hundreds of small sites have never been seen by archaeologists, and it is entirely possible that major sites still lie unreported. But within a generation or two, the forest will likely be gone; and, due to the predations of the looter—trafficking to the insatiable world art market—any new sites may well be devastated the instant they are discovered.[104]

Although no one can predict what the future will hold for the Mayans, the ancient priests predicted that the world will soon be drawing to an end. The great cycle of the Mayan calendar, which began on August 13, 3114 B.C., will come to an end after almost five thousand years on December 21, A.D. 2012. As written by the ancient priests, the date will read thirteen cycles, zero *katuns*, zero *tuns*, zero *uinals*, and zero *kins* since the beginning of the great cycle. On that day, 4 Ahau 3 Kankin, the prophecy, as written in *The Book of the Jaguar Priest*, reads,

> Then the sky is divided
> Then the land is raised,
> And then there begins
> The Book of the 13 Gods.
> Then occurs
> The great flooding of the Earth
> Then arises
> The great ltzam Cab Ain [creator].
> The ending of the world,
> The fold of the Katun:
> That is a flood
> Which will be the ending of the
>   world of the Katun.[105]

NOTES

Introduction: An Enduring Legacy

1. Gene S. Stuart and George E. Stuart, *Lost Kingdoms of the Maya*. Washington, DC: National Geographic Society, 1993, p. 13.

Chapter 1: Cities in the Forest

2. Robert J. Sharer, *Daily Life in Maya Civilization*. Westport, CT: Greenwood, 1996, p. 1.

3. Sharer, *Daily Life in Maya Civilization*, p. 2.

4. T. Patrick Culbert, *Maya Civilization*. Washington, DC: Smithsonian Books, 1993, p. 14.

5. Diego de Landa, *The Maya*, ed. and trans. by A. R. Pagden. Chicago: J. Philip O'Hara, 1975, p. 30.

6. Donald Ediger, *The Well of Sacrifice*. Garden City, NY: Doubleday, 1971, p. 39.

7. Robert J. Sharer, *The Ancient Maya*. Stanford, CA: Stanford University Press, 1994, p. 34.

8. Culbert, *Maya Civilization*, p. 19.

9. Quoted in Victor W. von Hagen, *Maya Explorer*. San Francisco: Chronicle Books, 1983, p. 97.

10. Quoted in Robert Wauchope, ed., *They Found Buried Cities*. Chicago: University of Chicago Press, 1974, pp. 81–82.

11. Dale M. Brown, ed., *The Magnificent Maya*. Alexandria, VA: Time-Life Books, 1993, p. 30.

12. Michael D. Coe, *Breaking the Maya Code*. New York: Thames and Hudson, 1992, p. 100.

13. Brown, *The Magnificent Maya*, p. 16.

14. Coe, *Breaking the Maya Code*, p. 110.

15. Stuart and Stuart, *Lost Kingdoms of the Maya*, p. 32.

16. Arthur A. Demarest, "The Violent Saga of a Maya Kingdom," *National Geographic*, February 1993, pp. 99–100.

Chapter 2: The Classic Mayan Civilization

17. Culbert, *Maya Civilization*, p. 46.

18. Culbert, *Maya Civilization*, pp. 50–51.

19. Linda Schele and Mary Miller, *The Blood of Kings: Dynasty and Ritual in Maya Art*. Fort Worth, TX: Kimball Art Museum, 1986, p. 300.

20. Sharer, *Daily Life in Maya Civilization*, pp. 157–58.

21. Delia Goetz and Sylvanus G. Morley, eds., *Popul Vuh*. Norman: University of Oklahoma Press, 1978, p. 167.

22. Culbert, *Maya Civilization*, pp. 58–59.

23. Culbert, *Maya Civilization*, p. 60.

24. C. Bruce Hunter, *A Guide to Ancient Maya Ruins*. Norman: University of Oklahoma Press, 1977, pp. 135, 138, 143.

25. Brown, *The Magnificent Maya*, p. 70.

26. Sharer, *Daily Life in Maya Civilization*, p. 55.

27. Sharer, *Daily Life in Maya Civilization*, pp. 55–56.

28. Victor W. von Hagen, *The Ancient Sun Kingdoms of the Americas*. Cleveland: World, 1961, pp. 346–47.

29. Ralph Whitlock, *Everyday Life of the Maya*. New York: Dorset, 1987, p. 82, 84.

30. Brown, *The Magnificent Maya*, p. 96.

Chapter 3: The Divine Kings

31. George E. Stuart, "The Royal Crypts of Copán," *National Geographic*, December 1997, p. 79, 80.

32. Culbert, *Maya Civilization*, p. 78.

33. Stuart, "The Royal Crypts of Copán," p. 82.

34. Davíd Carrasco, *Religions of Mesoamerica*. San Francisco: Harper & Row, 1990, p. 105.

35. Schele and Miller, *The Blood of Kings*, p. 66.

36. Schele and Miller, *The Blood of Kings*, p. 136.

37. Schele and Miller, *The Blood of Kings*, pp. 41–42.

38. Schele and Miller, *The Blood of Kings*, p. 43.

39. De Landa, *The Maya*, p. 82.

40. Carrasco, *Religions of Mesoamerica*, pp. 111–12.

41. Schele and Miller, *The Blood of Kings*, pp. 220–21.

42. Schele and Miller, *The Blood of Kings*, pp. 267–68.

43. Goetz and Morley, *Popul Vuh.*, p. 117.

44. Schele and Miller, *The Blood of Kings*, p. 274.

Chapter 4: Living by the Stars

45. Quoted in Howard La Fay, "The Maya, Children of Time," *National Geographic*, December 1975, p. 738.

46. La Fay, "The Maya, Children of Time," p. 729.

47. Sharer, *The Ancient Maya*, p. 560.

48. Berthold Riese, "The Star System," *UNESCO Courier*, November 1993, p. 22.

49. Quoted in La Fay, "The Maya, Children of Time," p. 749.

50. Sharer, *The Ancient Maya*, p. 562.

51. Stuart and Stuart, *Lost Kingdoms of the Maya*, p. 176.

52. Stuart and Stuart, *Lost Kingdoms of the Maya*, p. 176.

53. Sharer, *The Ancient Maya*, p. 567.

54. Culbert, *Maya Civilization*, pp. 36–37.

55. Maud Worcester Makemson, ed., *The Book of the Jaguar Priest*. New York: Henry Schuman, 1951, p. 140.

56. Schele and Miller, *The Blood of Kings*, p. 113.

57. John B. Carlson, "America's Ancient

Skywatchers," *National Geographic*, March 1990, p. 89.

58. Carlson, "America's Ancient Sky-watchers," p. 101.

59. Carlson, "America's Ancient Sky-watchers," p. 102.

60. Sharer, *The Ancient Maya*, p. 524.

61. Sharer, *The Ancient Maya*, p. 524.

62. Stuart and Stuart, *Lost Kingdoms of the Maya*, p. 178.

63. Michiel Berger, "Politics/Cosmology," Maya Astronomy Page, February 13, 1996. www.michielb.nl/maya/astro.html.

64. Schele and Miller, *The Blood of Kings*, p. 269.

65. Riese, "The Star System," p. 23.

Chapter 5: Daily Life

66. Quoted in La Fay, "The Maya, Children of Time," p. 746.

67. Sharer, *Daily Life in Maya Civilization*, p. 114.

68. Whitlock, *Everyday Life of the Maya*, pp. 33–35.

69. De Landa, *The Maya*, pp. 66–67.

70. Whitlock, *Everyday Life of the Maya*, pp. 39–40.

71. De Landa, *The Maya*, p. 72.

72. Sharer, *Daily Life in Maya Civilization*, p. 117.

73. Von Hagen, *The Ancient Sun Kingdoms of the Americas*, p. 241.

74. Quoted in La Fay, "The Maya, Children of Time," p. 749.

75. Culbert, *Maya Civilization*, p. 59.

76. Von Hagen, *The Ancient Sun Kingdoms of the Americas*, p. 254.

77. De Landa, *The Maya*, p. 92.

78. Von Hagen, *The Ancient Sun Kingdoms of the Americas*, pp. 255–56.

79. Von Hagen, *The Ancient Sun Kingdoms of the Americas*, pp. 264–65.

80. Von Hagen, *The Ancient Sun Kingdoms of the Americas*, p. 270–72.

81. Whitlock, *Everyday Life of the Maya*, p. 63.

82. Whitlock, *Everyday Life of the Maya*, pp. 60–61.

83. De Landa, *The Maya*, p. 69.

84. Goetz and Morley, *Popul Vuh*, p. 156.

85. De Landa, *The Maya*, pp. 69–70.

Chapter 6: The Decline and Fall of Mayan Civilization

86. Whitlock, *Everyday Life of the Maya*, p. 133.

87. Charles Gallenkamp, *Maya: The Riddle and Rediscovery of a Lost Civilization*. New York: David McKay, 1959, p. 154.

88. Sharer, *The Ancient Maya*, p. 338.

89. Sharer, *Daily Life in Maya Civilization*, p. 74.

90. Sharer, *The Ancient Maya*, p. 343.

91. Sharer, *The Ancient Maya*, p. 345.

92. Sharer, *The Ancient Maya*, p. 346.

93. Sharer, *The Ancient Maya*, pp. 348–49.

94. Brown, *The Magnificent Maya*, p. 126.

95. Sharer, *The Ancient Maya*, p. 383.

96. Makemson, *The Book of the Jaguar Priest*, p. 15.

97. Sharer, *The Ancient Maya*, p. 396.
98. Gallenkamp, *Maya*, p. 202.
99. Brown, *The Magnificent Maya*, pp. 145–46.
100. De Landa, *The Maya*, p. 45.
101. Brown, *The Magnificent Maya*, p. 150.

102. Von Hagen, *The Ancient Sun Kingdoms of the Americas*, p. 393.
103. Culbert, *Maya Civilization*, p. 19.
104. Culbert, *Maya Civilization*, p. 19.
105. Quoted in Coe, *Breaking the Maya Code*, p. 276.

FOR FURTHER READING

Dale M. Brown, ed., *The Magnificent Maya*. Alexandria, VA: Time-Life Books, 1993. This book explores the world of the ancient Mayans and the archaeologists, linguists, anthropologists, and others who uncovered the secrets of that society in the past centuries.

Irene Flum Galvin, *The Ancient Maya*. New York: Benchmark Books, 1997. Part of the Cultures of the Past series, this book is written for young adults about art, language, science, religion, and other aspects of ancient Mayan culture.

Delia Goetz and Sylvanus G. Morley, eds., *Popul Vuh*. Norman: University of Oklahoma Press, 1978. A modern translation of the sacred Quiché Maya council book first written by a Mayan nobleman in the sixteenth century. The book was translated by a Spanish friar, was then lost for several centuries, and was finally rediscovered in a Guatemalan library in the mid-1800s. Morley is one of the most highly respected authorities on Mayan civilization.

Linda Schele and Mary Miller, *The Blood of Kings: Dynasty and Ritual in Maya Art*. Fort Worth, TX: Kimball Art Museum, 1986. A large book with several hundred drawings and photos of Mayan hieroglyphs, pottery, sculpture, and other artwork accompanied by vivid and informative descriptions of each item and an explanation of the artwork's place in Mayan ritual and religion.

Robert J. Sharer, *Daily Life in Maya Civilization*. Westport, CT: Greenwood, 1996. An examination of daily life within the ancient Mayan empire. Written by a professor of anthropology and a researcher who lived and worked in Central America more than thirty years and wrote or edited more than twenty books on the Mayans.

John Lloyd Stephens, *Incidents of Travel in Yucatán*. Washington, DC: Smithsonian Institution, 1996. Originally published in 1843, this book details the incidents of hardship and the fascinating exploration of Mayan cities on the Yucatán Peninsula by Stephens and his companion Frederick Catherwood, the artist who illustrated the book with detailed drawings of the ruins in their original beauty before they were excavated by archaeologists.

Gene S. Stuart and George E. Stuart, *Lost Kingdoms of the Maya*. Washington, DC: National Geographic Society, 1993. An informative book with dozens of beautiful photos and interesting text by the experts at *National Geographic*.

Robert Wauchope, ed., *They Found Buried Cities*. Chicago: University of Chicago Press, 1974. Stories written by the original archaeological explorers in Mexico, Central America, and Peru. These first-hand accounts of scientific pioneers were written between 1805 and 1938 and contain a wealth of interesting—and sometimes bizarre—stories of men and women who suffered extreme hardships and risked their lives to uncover the mysteries of the ancient Mayans, Aztecs, Incas, and others.

Ralph Whitlock, *Everyday Life of the Maya*. New York: Dorset, 1987. A book that recreates the daily lives of the Mayan people, their beliefs, social hierarchy, ceremonies, literature, and science.

Periodicals

Arthur A. Demarest, "The Violent Saga of a Maya Kingdom," *National Geographic*, February 1993.

George E. Stuart, "The Royal Crypts of Copán," *National Geographic*, December 1997.

Websites

Maya Astronomy Page (www.michielb.nl/maya/astro.html). An excellent website maintained by Michiel Berger with separate pages containing information concerning Mayan mathematics, calendar systems, writing, astronomy, physical environment, the article "politics/cosmology," and links to related sites. Contains many graphics of numbers and hieroglyphs.

Maya Civilization—Past and Present (http://indy4.fdl.cc.mn.us/~isk/maya/maya.html). An excellent page with information about modern and ancient Mayan culture, language, numbers, maps, rain forest environment, curriculum, and links to over one hundred Mayan websites.

Works Consulted

Claude Baudez and Sydney Picasso, *Lost Cities of the Maya*. New York: Harry M. Abrams, 1992. Contains stories of the European explorers of Mayan lands from seventeenth-century Spanish priests to artists, photographers, and archaeologists in the nineteenth and twentieth centuries.

Davíd Carrasco, *Religions of Mesoamerica*. San Francisco: Harper & Row, 1990. A book in the Religious Traditions of the World series that explores the religious beliefs, mythologies, and creation stories of the Mayans, Aztecs, and other indigenous people of Mesoamerica.

Michael D. Coe, *Breaking the Maya Code*. New York: Thames and Hudson, 1992. Discusses the people and the research that helped decipher the ancient Mayan hieroglyphs whose meaning remained a mystery to researchers until the 1970s. The author is a professor of anthropology who worked with several of those who cracked the ancient code.

T. Patrick Culbert, *Maya Civilization*. Washington, DC: Smithsonian Books, 1993. Part of the Smithsonian Institution's Exploring the Ancient World series, this book examines the lost civilization of the Mayans from the earliest days of modern discovery down through the historic periods of the Mayan empire.

T. Patrick Culbert, ed., *The Classic Maya Collapse*. Albuquerque: University of New Mexico Press, 1977. A book of essays, written by thirteen leading Mayan scholars that studies the general collapse of that culture in the eighth and ninth centuries and attempts to answer questions surrounding the social and political fall of the Mayan civilization.

Donald Ediger, *The Well of Sacrifice*. Garden City, NY: Doubleday, 1971. An account of the expedition to the Sacred Cenote, or sacred well, on the Yucatán, where the Mayans sacrificed valuable objects and at least forty-two men, women, and children by drowning.

Charles Gallenkamp, *Maya: The Riddle and Rediscovery of a Lost Civilization*. New York: David McKay, 1959. A book written by a respected anthropologist and archaeologist who, as director of the Mayan Research Fund, studied the ancient Mayan culture on five separate archaeological expeditions.

Victor W. von Hagen, *The Ancient Sun Kingdoms of the Americas*. Cleveland: World, 1961. Discusses the history and cultural accomplishments of the Aztec, Mayan, and Inca peoples before the Spanish conquest. The author began his expeditions into the ancient sun kingdoms in 1930 and has written over forty books about Latin America's past.

———, *Maya Explorer*. San Francisco: Chronicle Books, 1983. An intriguing biography of "the Father of American Archaeology," John L. Stephens, who discovered the Mayan ruins at Copán in 1839 and spent the rest of his life attempting to decipher the secrets of that ancient civilization.

C. Bruce Hunter, *A Guide to Ancient Maya Ruins*. Norman: University of Oklahoma Press, 1977. An informative and complete tourist's guide to ancient ruins of Mexico and Central America.

Diego de Landa, *The Maya*. Ed. and trans. A. R. Pagden. Chicago: J. Philip O'Hara, 1975. The author was a sixteenth-century Spanish missionary who wrote about the Mayan people on the Yucatán Peninsula. This work, written in 1566 and discovered in 1864, is one of the only surviving sources that describes the customs, social organizations, and beliefs of the pre-Columbian Mayans.

Maud Worcester Makemson, ed., *The Book of the Jaguar Priest*. New York: Henry Schuman, 1951. This is an annotated translation of the *Book of Chilam Balam of Tizimin*, written during the time of the Spanish conquest by a few old Mayan shamans who could still remember the religious and cultural practices of past centuries.

Jeremy A. Sabloff, *The Cities of Ancient Mexico*. New York: Thames and Hudson, 1997. A book of short, descriptive literary sketches that tell what life was like in Mexico's greatest ancient cities during their glory days. Stories cover Mayan topics as well as Aztec and other native cultures.

Robert J. Sharer, *The Ancient Maya*. Stanford, CA: Stanford University Press, 1994. A comprehensive book, which reviewers call a classic, densely filled with information covering every aspect of the ancient Mayan culture. The author is a professor of anthropology and the curator of the American section of the University Museum of Archaeology and Anthropology at the University of Pennsylvania and has overseen numerous archaeological projects in the realm of the ancient Mayans.

Periodicals

John B. Carlson, "America's Ancient Skywatchers," *National Geographic*, March 1990.

Howard La Fay, "The Maya, Children of Time," *National Geographic*, December 1975.

Berthold Riese, "The Star System," *UNESCO Courier*, November 1993.

INDEX

Picture Credits

About the Author

Stuart A. Kallen is the author of over more than 150 nonfiction books for children and young adults. He has written on topics ranging from the theory of relativity to rock-and-roll history to life on the American frontier. In addition, Mr. Kallen has written award-winning children's videos and television scripts. In his spare time, Stuart A. Kallen is a singer/songwriter/guitarist in San Diego, California.